In the text, temperatures are given in Celsius. R
Fahrenheit thermometer may remember that .
equivalent of nine Fahrenheit degrees, while freezing is 0 degrees Celsius
and 32 degrees Fahrenheit. Some equivalents are listed below:

C	F
-70°	-94°
-50°	-58°
-40°	-40°
-35°	-31°
0°	+32°
+5°	+41°
+10°	+50°
+15°	+59°
+35°	+95°

Introduction

Part Three: Expanding Horizons

INTRODUCTION

F or five thousand years, the Eskimos, or *Inuit*, have survived in one of the harshest environments in the world, the Arctic. Here, at the top of the world, hardship and suffering go hand in hand with fortitude and courage. A mere fifty years ago, starvation, cannibalism and female infanticide were as much a part of their lives as hamburgers and electronic arcade games are today.

This transition from Stone Age to Space Age living, and its implications for the future, has passed almost unnoticed in the south. Although hundreds of books have been written about the Arctic, the majority allude to the courage of explorers, and by inference to that of their authors, who have consistently portrayed the Eskimo as 'Nanook of the North', the happy hunter living with his family and a litter of husky puppies in an igloo. *The Fourth World* is an attempt to destroy this outdated image.

Today, the old hunting culture is threatened by hydro-electric plants, oil pipelines, offshore oil rigs, western consumer goods and fall-out from military and political manoeuvering. In the next decade, and during the early years of the twenty-first century, industrial man will build new towns, roads, railways and airports in the frozen wastelands. Crops will be grown where previously there was only ice and snow. Ships, escorted by nuclear icebreakers, will regularly ply the Northwest and Northeast Passages, for centuries the dream of European merchants. On the polar ice cap, oil men will drill to a depth of 20,000 feet, while beneath them nuclear submarines bristling with missiles patrol the ocean darkness.

If, in the future, the Arctic is to be developed responsibly, it is important to review the effects on Eskimo culture of the developed world. This can be achieved only by studying and understanding the reasons for ancient Eskimo customs. To this end, Part One traces the Eskimo migrations from Siberia to Alaska, Canada and Greenland, and from the reports of the earliest travellers from the 'civilised' world shows how the Eskimos lived, and pieces together the fundamental reasons for their ability to survive.

The attitudes of the explorers, missionaries, whalers, hunters, trappers and traders, whose incursions contributed directly to the erosion of the Eskimo culture, are discussed in Part Two. This goes on to describe from personal observation the realities of the Arctic today, and to compare the plight of the Eskimos with that of the Sami (Lapps) of Scandinavia. Part Three deals with the new political awareness that is emerging among minority groups in the North, and looks at the future dangers and challenges in the Arctic.

Progress in all areas has been rapid and unchecked. Governments and business interests have exploited the region without thought for the land or the sea, or for the peoples of the north. In the scramble to exploit arctic riches, the 'Eskimos', whom we now know as 'Inuit', have been swept aside to become second-class citizens in their own territory. Since the Arctic was opened up during the 1940s, ignorance and greed have jeopardized the equilibrium not only of the delicate arctic environment, but of the entire northern hemisphere. Yet, once the wheels of the industrial mono-culture begin to turn, they are difficult to stop. They must, however, be brought under control at once if the Arctic is to be saved.

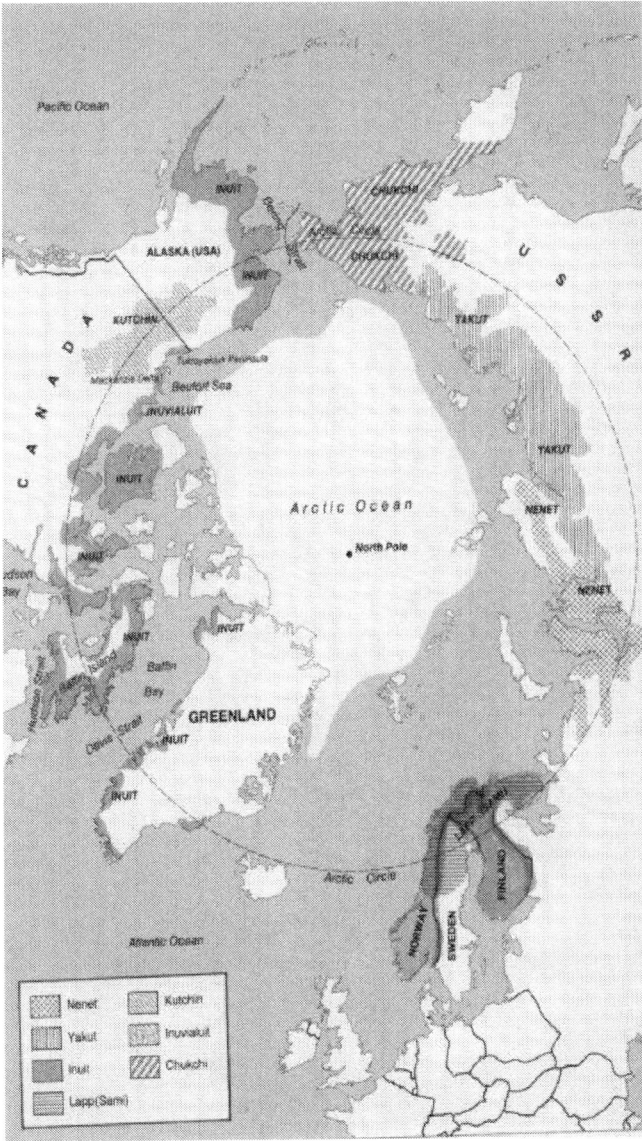

The Arctic and its Peoples   Swanston Graphics

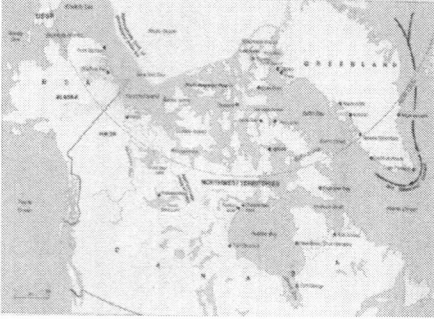

Greenland and the Canadian Arctic   Swanston Graphics

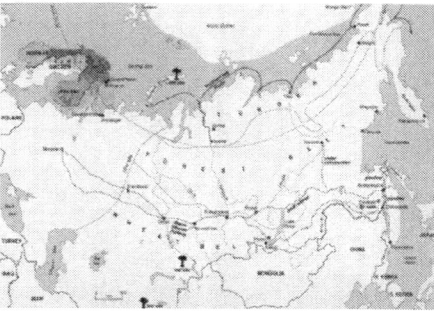

The Russian and Scandinavian Arctic   Swanston Graphics

ABOUT THE AUTHOR

Born in Cheshire, Sam Hall describes himself as a 'compulsive traveller'. As a young man he journeyed by bus, truck and train to Nepal. His journalistic career has taken him to nearly 70 countries, including Scandinavia where he lived for twelve years. As a Reuter correspondent in Stockholm, Miami and Lagos, and a reporter for Independent Television News, he covered the Nigerian-Biafran civil war and the Turkish invasion of Cyprus. His reports for *News at Ten* include the American hostages in Iran, riots in Paris, Amsterdam, Brixton and Tottenham, the Jeremy Thorpe trial, and the 1982 Siege of Beirut.An assignment to sail across the North Sea in a replica open Viking boat led him to deeper studies of the Vikings, on which he is now an expert. The Viking expansion westward later took him to the Faroe Islands, Iceland, Greenland and ultimately to the High Arctic. Whilst researching this book, he traveled thousands of miles throughout the Arctic in light aircraft, helicopters and boats, on skis skidoos, dog sleds and on foot. ITN screened a series of his special reports and his documentary *Greenland: The Vikings Return* was shown on Channel Four Television.

His other documentaries have won him several international awards, including Best Film of the Year in Norway, and Best Documentary of the Year in France. In recent years, he has been a guest speaker on many cruise ships, and in 2003, Britain's C.S. Media awarded him their Lifetime Achievement Award. Sam Hall is now 'retired'. He has a wife and three children and lives in Surrey.

About this book, he writes: "Unlike the uninhabited Antarctic, the lands and seas north of the Arctic Circle have sustained for thousands of years a native population – the Eskimos and the Lapps , or as we now know them, the Inuit and the Sami. These people lived by hunting or herding; they evolved a lifestyle of rigorous discipline and strong communal bonds without which they could not have survived in so implacably hostile an environment.

Then came the Europeans – explorers, traders, hunters, missionaries and administrators. With them came liquor, firearms, diseases; the arctic fauna started to be scientifically hunted into extinction. Later came the oil rigs, the Distant Early Warning line, the nuclear-rocket bunkers and the paraphernalia of World War Three; and in the old Soviet Union, the first of many an arctic megalopolis. The effect on the original people of the Arctic has been to destroy a traditional culture and set nothing valid in its place.

A nuclear reactor explodes in Russia; in Samiland, north of Norway, the reindeer, the chief livelihood of the population, faced extinction. The Greenland seals may have been protected, but not those for whom the seal has been the prime source of food, clothing, heat and light. The Inuit may have graduated from fermented walrus meat to canned frankfurters, and from dog sledges to snowmobiles – but their only real gain has been the beginnings of an urgent sense of nationalism and the desperation to pursue it by all legal means.

The whole world stands to suffer along with the native peoples of the Arctic. The polar regions serve to regulate the climate and ecology of the world's temperate zones; as the Arctic comes under threat from modern technology the consequence may be global disaster sooner than expected. In *The Fourth World* Sam Hall evokes the traditional lifestyle of the arctic peoples, describes the erosion of this culture under the impact of colonialism, and makes an indisputable case for a common collaboration to save the Arctic from further despoliation.

PART THREE

Expanding Horizons

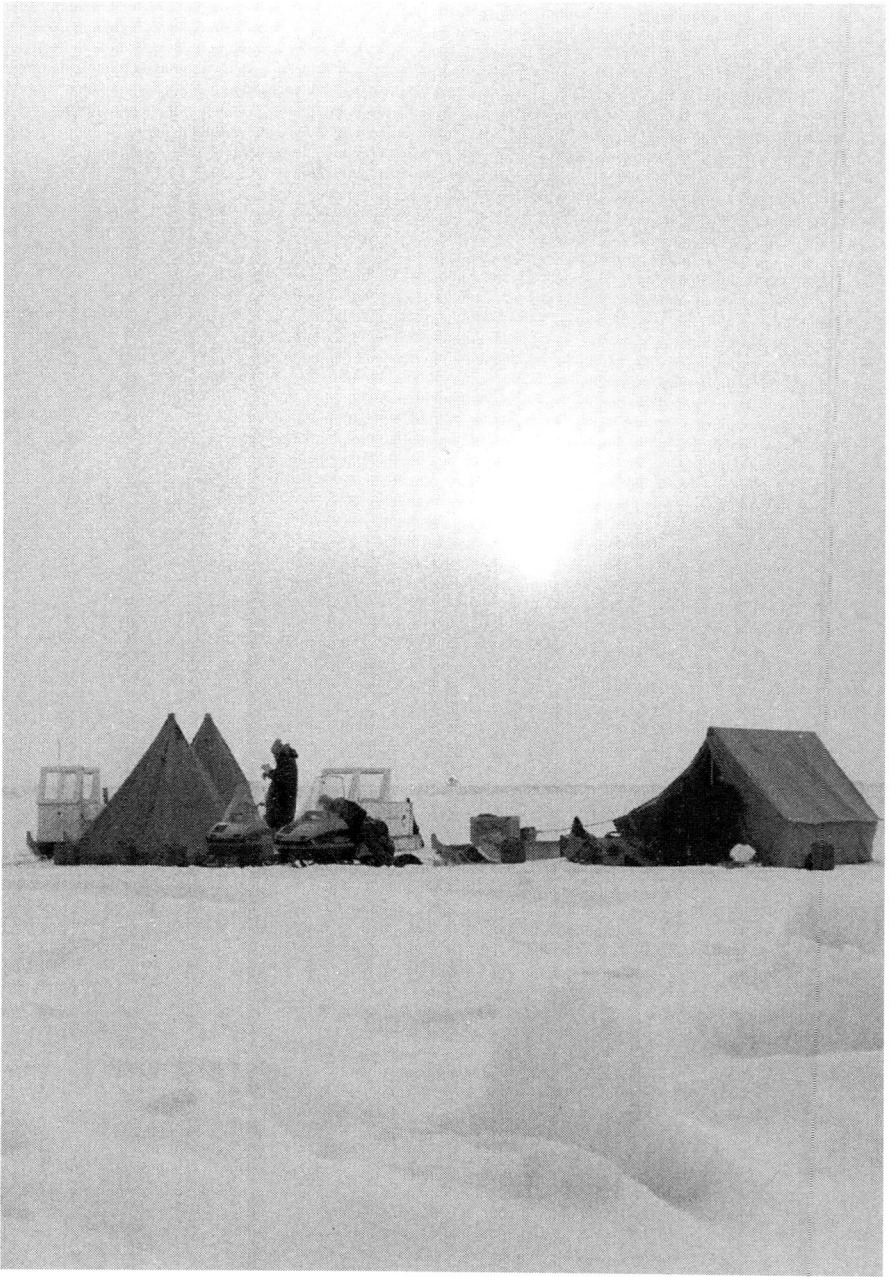

CHAPTER 1

The Road to Nunavut

From the earliest voyages of discovery and plunder, the *qallunaat* from the south seized ownership of the arctic lands, ignoring the rights of the indigenous populations. When American whalers informed the Inuit in 1867 that the United States government had purchased Alaska from the Russians for $7.2 million, the hunters could not believe that the land in which their forefathers had lived for 4,000, or perhaps 10,000 years, would belong to anyone but themselves. They had not been consulted, either by the Americans or by the Russians, nor were they offered compensation from the sale.

Such indifference towards the Inuit became accepted government practice, and they suffered in much the same way as the Aborigines, Maoris, Amerindians, Cossacks and other tribes around the world. Throughout the north, land that had been neither surrendered in war nor revoked in peace was purloined by various southern governments. The Russians, Americans, Canadians, British and Scandinavians each exploited the local resources, rehoused the inhabitants and imposed upon them their own customs and beliefs.

For years, the disgruntled Inuit and Sami stood by helplessly. There seemed to be no one capable or powerful enough to overcome the despair which shadowed the entire arctic region. Yet, such a man did exist. His name was Etok, better known as Charles Edwardsen, Jr. When the U.S. fleet arrived off the Alaskan coast in 1944 to establish a naval base near Barrow, effectively bringing Alaskan isolation to an end, Etok had barely celebrated his first birthday. The son of a whaler, his earliest memories were of the differences between the conditions of the hunters, who lived in poverty with no water supply, sewage system or clinic, and those of the sailors and government officials who enjoyed the benefits of electricity, radio, television, telephones and health care.

The contrast must have seemed greater still when he was sent 1,000 miles from his home to attend a government school in the south, where he studied in centrally-heated classrooms electrically lit. Here, he luxuriated in hot baths and learned how to use a porcelain lavatory, visited the cinema and listened to the radio. As his awareness sharpened, he began to understand the plight of the Inuit people, and learned to think like a *qallunaat*. In his early twenties, Etok decided to fight back.

Realising that the Inuit had never formally surrendered the Alaskan North Slope, which lay between the mountains of the Brooks Range and the arctic coast, Etok was convinced that the solution to the frustration and anger of his people was to win back the territory that had been taken from them. If the *qallunaat* wanted to use the land, he declared, let them pay for it.

Ironically, the U.S. Atomic Energy Commission provided the catalyst Etok needed to accomplish his aim. A plan to detonate an atomic bomb and to blast a deep-water port from the bedrock at Cape Thompson, near the Inuit village of Point Hope on the Alaskan coast, was causing serious concern and bitterness amongst the Inuit. Their counsel had not been sought.

Yet, contamination was expected to affect an area of nearly 50,000 square miles, with possibly devastating effects on the caribou, fish, sea mammals and birdlife upon which the Inuit were dependent for their livelihood. Local meetings were called, and Etok seized the opportunity to influence grassroots opinion on the wider issues. When details of the nuclear plan became widely known, public anger was so great that the Commission was forced to abandon the project.

A few months later, an Inuk named Johnnie Nusunginya was arrested for shooting a duck. Although he only wanted food for his family, the Inuk hunter had knowingly contravened an international treaty controlling the hunting of migratory birds. In specifying the hunting season, the legislators had concentrated on controlling the activities of sportsmen in the south and had ignored the Inuit in the north for whom ducks and geese were an essential supplement to their diet.

When the season opened legally in the autumn, most birds had flown south from the Arctic and would not return until spring, after the season had closed. If Johnnie Nusunginya and his fellow hunters wished to eat, they had no option but to disregard the law. As word spread of his arrest, 138 other Inuit took their guns, each bagged a duck, and presented themselves to the game warden for arrest. Eventually, all the charges were dropped.

Capitalising on these successes, Etok created the Arctic Slope Native Association (ASNA). He was aware that without a strong power base from which to fight a land claim, historical right counted for nothing. He therefore journeyed round Alaska to persuade other communities to form similar organisations. Stories of gas in the thin layer of earth above the permafrost spurred him on with an added sense of urgency. Despite many setbacks, he eventually welded Indian and Inuit local native associations into one body, the Alaska Federation of Natives (AFN).

Under this common umbrella, each member association formulated land claims based on past hunting traditions, and presented them to the authorities in Alaska and Washington. ASNA demanded virtually all of
the North Slope, an area totalling nearly sixty million acres. As events were to prove, this was not as pointless as many people at first believed. On July 18th, 1968, at Prudhoe Bay on the north coast of Alaska, the 51st and last exploration hole that British Petroleum and its partner, Atlantic Richfield, planned to drill into the North Slope, struck oil. Suddenly, Inuit land was worth money.

Prudoe Bay station processing oil for the Alaskan pipeline.

Within weeks, the boom was in full swing. Oil men, adventurers and speculators descended on the area. The State of Alaska auctioned drilling concessions covering 450,000 acres in Prudhoe Bay. The winning bid for one of the new oil leases was $272 million. In a single morning, the State of Alaska sold drilling rights for $900,220,590.21. Realising the potential for gaining public support throughout the United States, Etok and a few friends patrolled outside the salesroom, carrying placards which highlighted the poverty of the Inuit, and their helplessness in trying to tackle governments and multi-national oil companies. It was a story no journalist could ignore.

With the Inuit land-claims pending, the oil men were anxious to verify the legality of their leases before building a pipeline to carry the oil from Prudhoe Bay to Fairbanks. The Secretary for the Interior at the time, Steward Udall, believed that until the issue of land ownership had been settled by Congress, the transfer of federal land, and oil and gas leases should be frozen. In Washington, the administration was eager to reach a financial settlement under which native rights would be forsworn for all eternity, but Etok and his close associates were not interested in money. They wanted land, and control over its development. It was as if the Inuit negotiators were directing their infinite patience and hunting instincts towards a new quarry, the *qallunaat*.

After much wrangling, bitter in-fighting within the AFN, and some pressure from oil companies, Congress passed the Alaskan Native Claims Settlement Act of 1971. It allowed the natives to own outright 44 million acres, or approximately ten per cent, of the land in Alaska. In return for giving up the remainder, they received a cash payment of nearly a billion dollars.

In a referendum two years later, the Inuit elected to establish the North Slope as a borough, and imposed taxes of nearly seven million dollars on the oil companies and their property. At first, the oil men refused to accept the legality of the borough and contested the levy in the courts, but were overruled by the Alaskan Supreme Court.

By the time he had celebrated his thirtieth birthday, Etok finally achieved his aim and forced the *qallunaat* to pay for the use of Inuit land. He had seen a remarkable transformation in his homeland. In the North Slope villages, where during his childhood there had been a lack of sanitation and other amenities, there were now supplies of electricity and water, as well as sewage systems, schools, clinics, modern stores and satellite telephones. The price of victory, however, was high.

The ultimate intention of the Settlement Act had always been to absorb the Inuit into the mainstream culture, and in this it was spectacularly successful. Most of the billion-dollar compensation was used to underwrite more than 200 profit-making corporations, owned and administered by a new breed of Inuit executives and shareholders. Shouldering the mantle of capitalism, the guardians of these huge investments grew to be dependent not on the land, but on its continued exploitation, and as a result were thrown into conflict with the Inuit who wished to remain hunters.

Poorly advised by white consultants and cheated by sharp businessmen, the new tycoons made many mistakes. Improvement schemes were neglected and the towns for which there had been so much hope declined into ramshackle slums. In the end, Etok's idealism appeared to have produced little more than greed and corruption, discontent and discord, followed by boredom, endless hours of television, alcoholism, violence and crime.

In 1991, the Alaskan Inuit will be free to sell their land and compensation shares. Bids could be as high as a million dollars for each individual. Such wealth has left the Alaskan Inuit torn between two lifestyles, one desperately hoping to preserve the old hunting traditions, the other anxious to retain the modern advantages brought by the land claims and the oil. Whether the future encompasses the best of both worlds, or the worst, will depend mainly on whether there is a resurgence of native pride. That, in turn, may be decided by events in Canada, Greenland and Samiland.

In Canada, the discovery of oil at Prudhoe Bay had raised hopes that huge oil and gas reserves might exist in Canadian waters, especially in the Mackenzie Delta region of the Beaufort Sea. One obstacle to exploration, however, was the Arctic Island Preserve, an area of nearly 450,000 square miles of arctic territory reserved for Inuit use by a government order of 1926.

The order represented an early attempt by the Canadians to establish sovereignty over the Northwest Passage and the arctic islands further north, but it proved particularly useful four years later when the Norwegian government supported an application to extract minerals from the islands discovered by the Norwegian explorer, Otto Sverdrup.

The Canadians replied that they were unable to help because the area had been set aside for the exclusive use of the Inuit. Forty years on, and confident that oil would be found, the federal government in Ottawa quickly thrust aside such sentiments, repealed the order and began to issue exploration concessions.

With the prospect of an oil bonanza dawning in the north, a regional government was established at Yellowknife, the capital of the Northwest Territories. It came under the authority of the Department of Indian Affairs and Northern Development (DIAND), whose dual, and conflicting, role was to assist industrial development, and at the same time safeguard the social well-being of the native people. The administrators of DIAND left no doubt as to their interpretation of the latter responsibility; the sooner the Indians and Inuit were assimilated into the Canadian culture the better, a view shared wholeheartedly by the Prime Minister, Pierre Trudeau.

The Mackenzie Delta Inuit, still recovering from the devastating effects of their encounters with American whalers at the turn of the century, realised that decisions vital to their future were being made without their knowledge. Fearful that their aboriginal rights would be swept away in a tidal wave of development, a blind Inuk called Sam Raddi hastily formed the Committee for Original Peoples' Entitlement (COPE), the first political organisation of its kind in Canada. Raddi, inspired by the successes of the Alaskan Inuit, wasted no time raising the question of land ownership.

With equal speed, Ottawa rejected the whole concept of aboriginal rights. The federal government declared that the land claims were so vague as to be questionable in law. In British Columbia, Pierre Trudeau asserted that everybody in Canada, no matter what their origins, should be equal. A single social group, he said, could not make a separate deal with the rest of society.

If the Indians and Inuit were saying that they wanted to re-negotiate previous 'beads for land' agreements because they considered that they had been cheated, then so far as he was concerned, they were wasting their time. The past could not be redeemed. Instead of seeking aboriginal rights, the Prime Minister declared, they should accept that their first duty was to become Canadian, and be treated like everyone else.

Thrusting Inuit fears aside and without consulting the public, the government pushed ahead with its plans to develop the north. Lucrative tax incentives were offered to drilling companies prepared to risk exploration in the Beaufort Sea. The government insisted that these did not necessarily give them the right to extract and transport oil, but companies spending tens of millions of dollars on exploratory drilling had a powerful argument on their side. In the meantime, they could write off as much as 200 per cent of their costs. Within two years of the Prudhoe Bay discovery, the government had issued nearly 10,000 exploration permits and 450 oil leases covering 450 million acres of Inuit land.

Throngs of drilling teams descended on the Mackenzie Delta. They punched more than a hundred holes into the subsoil" and soon found an abundance of natural gas, and later, oil. The Minister for Energy declared that there were gas reserves for 330 years, and supplies of oil for more than 920 years, enough for themselves, and plenty more for export to the United States.

Alarmed by the rapid turn of events, the Indians and Inuit realised that their only hope was to negotiate from a stronger, national political base. With this in mind, they formed the Inuit Tapirisat of Canada (lTC), or the Inuit Brotherhood. In the course of time, the Inuit organisation was to become a major political force, run on government grants of a million dollars a year, and an equal amount in interest-free loans against future land claim settlements.

Although partially funded by the government, the ITC did not become subservient to the administration. One of the first lessons the Inuit leaders and their advisers learned was the importance of public relations. Lambasting the government at each hint of unfair treatment, they gained nationwide publicity.

Soon, a group of independent and distinguished engineers, lawyers, scientists and businessmen, concerned about the threat to the arctic environment and Inuit culture, founded a watchdog organisation, the Canadian Arctic Resources Committee. Its purpose was to promote a balanced and responsible approach to development, to protect the north and to respect the rights of the Inuit to take part in decision making. From now on, the government had to tread more carefully.

Pierre Trudeau's forceful declaration had stunned both the Indians and the Inuit. The Nishga Indians of British Columbia argued that Canada had adopted the British judicial system, and that as British law recognised native population rights, the whole question of aboriginal rights should be tested in court. They had signed no treaties with the Canadians, and in the writ served on the provincial government they demanded that recognition must be given to their original right to the land in Nass River Valley, where their people had lived for centuries.

The case proved historic. Although the Indians lost, and the Court of Appeal upheld the ruling, six judges of the Supreme Court were evenly divided. The seventh dismissed the case on a technicality, but agreed that the Indians did have aboriginal rights, and that they had never lost them by legal means. Pierre Trudeau was quick to appreciate the significance of the ruling, which was effectively a victory by a vote of four to three for the Indians. Two weeks later, the government changed course.

Reluctantly accepting that compensation should be paid where traditional interests were adversely affected, the government let it be known that it was ready to negotiate, and vested large amounts of money in native organisations to help them fight their cause. Three months after the Nishga ruling, talks began with representatives of 7,500 Cree Indians and 4,500 Inuit living in northern Quebec to settle what was known as the James Bay dispute.

T   he James Bay hydro-electric project was an ambitious three-phase plan to regulate seven major rivers flowing into the east side of James Bay, some of them the largest in North America. Costing nearly $6 billion for the first phase alone, this was the largest civil engineering project in Canadian history. It was intended to probe 500 miles into the heartland of northern Quebec in a series of ten artificial lakes and more than 200 dams, with power stations, access roads and airports. The scheme would satisfy the growing demand for electricity in eastern American cities for the foreseeable future. It would generate thirty per cent of the power produced in Canada, and more than one-tenth of North America's total electricity consumption.

Although hordes of southern workers were to be assigned to the area and vast tracts of land would be flooded, the Indians and Inuit were ignored, and learned of the project only by hearsay. There had been no serious attempt to study the damage such a massive scheme might cause to the environment. Bewildered, the Cree and the Inuit, like the Nishga Indians, also turned to the courts for help.

Seeking the aid of sympathetic lawyers, they applied for an injunction to halt work on the project. They argued that the scheme was in violation of their native rights and would disrupt the ecological balance of the region irrevocably. After a year of testimony and deliberation, the court ruled that changing the flow of the rivers, eroding their beds and banks, and flooding adjacent areas on such a vast scale meant that the native people would no longer be able to hunt, trap or fish in the affected areas, and granted an injunction until the issue of native rights had been settled.

The victory was short-lived. Eight days later, an Appeals Court overturned the decision. Nevertheless, the provincial government was worried that work on the project might be stopped by further appeals, and no doubt mindful of the Nishga Indian ruling three months earlier, agreed to talk.

A year of hard bargaining followed, and eventually the two sides reached an agreement in principle. The Indians and Inuit were not at all happy with the proposed deal, which had been hammered out with maximum haste and under considerable pressure from the developers. Like the Alaska Native Claims Act, it amounted to little more than an exchange of ancestral land and hunting rights for cash, with a package of social programmes thrown in for good measure.

Adopting a tough stance, the provincial government negotiators intimated that the native groups could take the offer or leave it. They warned that work on the project would continue irrespective of whether they signed the agreement or not, and added that an appeal to the Supreme Court would be prohibitively expensive and could take up to ten years to settle. By that time, the project would have been completed, and the native groups would have gained nothing.

With their backs to the wall, the Cree and the Inuit accepted $225 million compensation, the right of ownership to 1.3 per cent of their territory, and exclusive hunting, fishing and whaling rights to 14 per cent of the land. Viewed from the opposite standpoint, the James Bay Agreement had deprived them of 98.7 per cent of their native land, and 86 per cent of their hunting and fishing rights in return for approximately $18,750 for each individual. This amount was payable over several years, and depreciated rapidly owing to subsequent inflation. Nevertheless, the agreement was better than nothing and an important lesson for Inuit elsewhere.

As the details of the James Bay agreement were being thrashed out, another development project was announced which threatened to have an even greater impact on Indian and Inuit affairs. This was a plan to build a $10 billion pipeline to transport gas from Prudhoe Bay along the north coast of Alaska and Yukon to the Mackenzie Delta. Here, it would link up with Canadian gas fields before snaking south through the Mackenzie Valley to join an American pipeline system in Alberta, a total distance of 2,625 miles.

Conservationists were particularly concerned about the inadequacies of a new government review process, which required the effects on the environment to be gauged before construction started. Although the government had laid down set guidelines, responsibility for the inquiry, and the method of assessment, was left to the firms involved. Company experts were frequently more highly qualified than the government employees who scrutinised the final reports and made the recommendations upon which a final decision would be based.

It was also in the interests of developers to isolate the various aspects of a project when weighing its possibly damaging effects. A firm appraising the potential harm to the ecology from a pipeline might consider it in their own interests to conduct a separate assessment on the pumping stations. Similarly, a multinational company could concentrate on the detrimental features of a single drilling rig, fully aware that if oil was discovered the impact from a multitude of wells, pumping stations, pipelines, roads and increased ground and air traffic would be infinitely greater.

Feeling threatened by the Mackenzie Valley pipeline, the Indian and Inuit Brotherhoods lobbied urgently for a public inquiry. At the same time, the Canadian Arctic Resources Committee detailed the likely hazards of the scheme. Sympathy groups protested and the southern press rounded on the government, which had been extraordinarily secretive about its development policies for the north, particularly with regard to the granting of exploration permits and oil leases, and the publication of research work. With the growing dissent posing a potential security risk to the expensive and vulnerable pipeline, the government capitulated, and appointed a widely respected Supreme Court judge from British Columbia, Thomas Berger, to head the inquiry.

J udge Berger approached his task earnestly, and with refreshing probity.

He listened to everyone who had anything to say. He travelled thousands of miles to visit witnesses who were unable to attend the main hearings in Yellowknife. In all, he heard testimony from 3,000 experts and 1,000 local inhabitants in nearly fifty towns, villages and settlements, and collected 33,353 pages of evidence. Never before had such attention been paid to the native viewpoint, nor had it been so widely publicised.

As Judge Berger journeyed across the country, he realised that the land which the government and the developers regarded only as a frontier to be conquered was a home for those who lived there. The local people were not interested in cash compensation. They wanted to keep their land and determine their own futures, and they begged for time to consider how they might protect their cultures while trying to adjust to the inexorable advance of development.

Greatly moved by the overwhelming opposition to the project, Judge

Berger stressed in his findings the importance of protecting animal and birdlife, particularly the huge caribou herds and the snow geese. He suggested that instead of building a pipeline which would dissect the migratory routes of the caribou in north Yukon, the government should create a national park, in which the native population should be granted sovereign hunting rights. Finally, he recommended that the pipeline through the Mackenzie Valley should be postponed for ten years to enable native land claims to be settled before construction work began. On publication of the report, the Indians and Inuit were jubilant. In Ottawa, the government was appalled.

During the early days of the inquiry, the Indians had refused to negotiate with the federal Land Claims Office on the grounds that their land, the whole of the Northwest Territories south of the tree line from the Mackenzie River to Hudson Bay, was not for sale. Refuting the government view that the James Bay Agreement was a precedent for the settlement of all other land claims, they emphasised that their people had lived in *Denendeh*, meaning 'The Land of the People', for 30,000 years. They had no intention of relinquishing it now for what they considered to be yet another trinkets-and-blankets-for-land agreement.

Consequently, at a meeting of the Indian Brotherhood at Fort Simpson in July 1975, 300 delegates voted unanimously to adopt an historic document called 'The Dene Declaration'. For the government, which had seen its relations with six million French-speaking Canadians in Quebec deteriorate almost to the point of secession, the opening sentence verged on treason. It stated:

> We the Dene of the Northwest Territories insist on the right to be regarded by ourselves and the world as a nation.

The document continued, with touching simplicity:

> Our struggle is for the recognition of the Dene Nation by the government and people of Canada and the peoples and governments of the world. As once Europe was the exclusive homeland of the European peoples, Africa the exclusive homeland of the African peoples, the New World, North and South America, was the exclusive homeland of Aboriginal peoples of the New World, the Amerindian and the Inuit.

The New World like other parts of the world has suffered the experience of colonialism and imperialism. Other peoples have occupied the land - often with force - and foreign governments have imposed themselves on our people. Ancient civilizations and ways of life have been destroyed.

Colonialism and imperialism is now dead or dying. Recent years have witnessed the birth of new nations or rebirth of old nations out of the ashes of colonialism.

As Europe is the place where you will find European countries with European governments for European peoples, now also you will find in Africa and Asia the existence of African and Asian countries with African and Asian governments for the African and Asian people.

The African and Asian peoples - the peoples of the Third World - have fought for and won the right to self-determination, the right to recognition as distinct peoples and the recognition of themselves as nations.

But in the New World the Native peoples have *not* fared so well. Even in countries in South America where the native peoples are the vast majority of the population there is not one country which has an Amerindian government for the Amerindian peoples. Nowhere in the New World have the Native peoples won the right to self-determination and the right to recognition by the world as a distinct people and as nations. While the Native people of Canada are a minority in their homeland, the Native people of the N.W.T., the Dene and the Inuit, are a majority of the population of the N.W.T.

The Dene find themselves as part of a country. That country is Canada. But the Government of Canada is not the government of the Dene. The Government of the N.W.T. is not the government of the Dene. These governments were not the choice of the Dene, they were imposed upon the Dene.

What we the Dene are struggling for is the recognition of the Dene Nation by the governments and peoples of the world.

And while there are realities we are forced to submit to, such as the existence of a country called Canada, we insist on the right to self-determination as a distinct people and the recognition of the Dene Nation.

We the Dene are part of the Fourth World. And as the peoples and nations of the world have come to recognize the existence and rights of those peoples who make up the Third World the day must come and will come when the nations of the Fourth World will come to be recognized and respected. The challenge to the Dene and the world is to find the way for the recognition of the Dene Nation.

Our plea to the world is to help us in our struggle to find a place in the world community where we can exercise our right to selfdetermination as a distinct people and a nation.

What we seek then is independence and self-determination within the country of Canada. This is what we mean when we call for a just settlement for the Dene Nation.

The Dene Declaration was a milestone. It created new hope for the Dene, and inspired the Inuit. Shortly afterwards, the Dene placed their relationship with the government on an entirely new footing by formally submitting a proposal for local government which would control land resources and nature conservation. Although it was repeatedly emphasised that self-determination would be within the framework of the Confederation, many Canadians viewed the proposal as a threat of secession. Pierre Trudeau refused to accept what he called an autonomous native local government based on race. The proposal is still being negotiated.

The Inuit, who had been discussing their own claims along the lines of the Alaska Native Claims Settlement Act and the James Bay Agreement, decided to withdraw from the negotiations, and begin again. Starting from the premise that their right to self-determination had never been surrendered, they pressed for political power as well as compensation for past wrongs.

Although there were no academics in their ranks, the accurate documentation of their culture was vital if critics were to be convinced that their way of life was, and always had been, inextricably bound up with vast areas of the arctic environment. With the help of the anthropologist Milton Freeman, virtually every adult hunter in the Canadian Arctic was questioned about his hunting journeys, equipment and methods. Wildlife patterns were charted and hunting grounds mapped with infinite detail. It was the most complete description of Inuit life ever undertaken.

Freeman's three-volume report proved not only that during their lifetime, many Inuit hunters travelled between 10,000 and 20,000 miles on hunting trips, but that they had occupied every part of the Arctic for at least 4,000 years, and were therefore justified in claiming ownership of approximately 770,000 square miles of land and 865,000 square miles of sea as their home.

Heartened by the Alaskan settlement and the progress made on their home front, the Mackenzie Delta Inuit, known as the Inuvialuit, negotiated a special agreement with the government. Under it, they were guaranteed 35,000 square miles of land in perpetuity, with mineral rights to 18 per cent of it, and nearly $120 million (£60 million) compensation. Both land and cash were placed in trust so that there could be no question of selling out, as in Alaska.

Clearly influenced by the Dene Declaration, other Inuit stressed in a similar document that as they had never had a constitutional relationship with the Canadian government, they wished to form a new territory within the Canadian Confederation, to be governed by themselves under the supervision of Ottawa. It must contain all the land and sea north of the Canadian tree line, an area the size of India. They called it Nunavut, the Inuktitut word for 'Our Land'.

The concept of a Dene Nation and Nunavut made sense. The new territories would separate the histories, ultures and climates of the two peoples along a natural border, with the Dene occupying the forests to the south of the tree line, and the Inuit the tundra and arctic wastelands further north. It was not a question of creating separate ethnic states, but the fervent desire of the Dene and the Inuit to govern themselves, rather than be ruled by southern administrators who did not fully understand their problems, and whose seat of government at Yellowknife was hundreds of miles from many of the isolated areas whose future they were trying to decide.

Ottawa's reaction to the Nunavut proposal was predictable. Insisting that autonomous native governments based on race could not be discussed in the same context as land claims, the federal government reiterated that the James Bay Agreement was a precedent from which it would not depart. With negotiations deadlocked and the Northwest Territories in political turmoil, Pierre Trudeau attempted to cool the situation by appointing a former cabinet minister, Charles Drury, to investigate the possibility of constitutional reform in the north. Drury, however, was boycotted by native groups and the inquiry was an embarrassing political failure.

Nobody seemed to notice that the Drury report included a recommendation that the Northwest Territories should ultimately be divided into two parts, a suggestion which was subsequently endorsed in a referendum, and tentatively approved by the federal government in Ottawa. Today, the dream of Nunavut is a

reality. All the land and sea north of the Canadian tree line is governed by autonomous Inuit rule, whilst still remaining within the Canadian Confederation and under the supervision of Ottowa. The Canadian government, for all its initial dithering, is to be commended for this landmark advance.

CHAPTER 2

Fighting Back

Approaching *Prince Leopold Island, Canadian Arctic.*
Author's photograph

The Nunavut proposal sparked a renewed sense of pride among the Canadian Inuit. During a visit to North America in September, 1984, Pope John Paul II gave them what they needed more than anything else initial recognition of the justice of their battle for self-determination. Apologising for the heavy-handed evangelising of previous Catholic missionaries, he unequivocally expressed solidarity with Canada's native people, and told thousands of Indians and Inuit at St Anne de Beaupre in Quebec: 'You must be the architects of your own future, freely and responsibly.' Pope John Paul added that further progress was needed, and said this should be negotiated 'in the increased recognition of your own decision-making power'. Afterwards, Stephen Kakfwi, the President of the Dene Nation, described the visit as the beginning of a new era.

In fact, the new era had already begun when large numbers of Inuit children were sent during the post-war period to be educated in the south. Like Etok, many of them subsequently returned home to fight the cause of their people, quickly gaining experience from government negotiations, legal actions and contacts with sympathetic liberal groups. The emerging leaders also maintained informal contacts with the Alaskan Inuit, and had been inspired by the events in Greenland where the Inuit had made even greater progress.

Here, like a phoenix rising from the ashes of despair, the Inuit leadership had managed to shrug off its disillusionment, and wrested from the Danes the most comprehensive form of self-determination anywhere in the Arctic. This change in their fortunes stemmed from a decision to amend the Danish constitution in 1953. Until then, Greenland had been a Danish crown colony, governed centrally from Copenhagen. Now, it was to become an equal and integral part of the Danish Kingdom, with the Inuit representatives occupying two of the 179 seats in the Danish *Folketing*, or parliament.

Denmark's vision for the future of Greenland was a simple one. In a country where there was no agriculture or forestland, and minerals were difficult to extract, economic viability hinged on the enormous stocks of cod and shrimp off the west coast. The fishing industry would have to be modernised, fish factories built, and the hunting communities moved into the towns. Housing would be needed to accommodate the influx of people, schools would have to be provided to educate them, and hospitals to treat their illnesses.

The Danes paid for all of it. They decided that if the young Inuit were to become wage-earners in the modern industrialised society, it was essential that they be taught the Danish language, but until they achieved fluency, Greenland would have to import Danish labour.

One difficulty was the necessity to offer high salaries to Danish workers to induce them to work in the Arctic. If Inuit labourers were paid equally well, the high cost could negate the whole purpose of the experiment, which was to nurse the country to economic health. The *Folketing* solved this dilemma by enacting a law which permitted Danes to be paid higher salaries than the Inuit for exactly the same jobs.

Appreciating the need for progress, many Inuit politicians supported the Danish approach and reluctantly accepted the discriminatory pay law as a necessary evil, but the majority of the population voiced their intense displeasure. In their view, the Danish dream was a recipe for disaster, and their complaints did not go unheard.

In the municipal councils, a new breed of politician was emerging. These were the Inuit leaders who dissociated themselves from policies which forced hunters to abandon their hunting traditions, and humiliated their people with inferior wages. They were angered that Danish was the principal teaching medium in the schools and outraged that students should be obliged to travel to Denmark for further education. Seeing no gain in centralising the population, they rebelled against the control wielded by the Danes over every aspect of their lives.

The new political generation pictured the Danish dream as a nightmare in which the Greenlandic language, community spirit and Inuit culture were slowly being extinguished. Soon, these angry young Inuit would become the elected representatives to the Provincial Council, the national advisory body to the Danish *Folketing*. Eventually, their voices would be heard in the *Folketing* itself, and in time, they would achieve what no Inuk had dared to believe possible.

As Etok negotiated the final draft of the Alaska Native Claims Act, and the Cree and Canadian Inuit sought to stop the James Bay project, three Greenlanders, a poet, a teacher and a clergyman, joined together and became a formidable political force. The poet, Moses Olsen, agitated for the opportunity to let Greenlanders solve their own problems. The teacher, Lars EmilJohansen, warned of cultural genocide at the hands of the Danes, and Jonathan Motzfeldt, the clergyman, demanded the abolition of the discriminatory pay policy. The three men sat on Greenland's Provincial Council, and two of them, Olsen and Johansen, were elected to the Danish *Folketing*. In 1973, Jonathan Motzfeldt formally demanded that the Greenlanders be granted Home Rule.

The Danes were stunned. The Copenhagen government could not conceive that the vast amounts of money spent on helping Greenland into the modern world was in anything but the best interests of the Inuit. Many Danes publicly denounced them for being ungrateful. Deeply wounded and genuinely concerned that its good intentions might have been misguided, the government eventually set up a commission to discuss the issue. The numbers were evenly divided between Danes and Greenlanders, the first time the Inuit had been accepted on an equal basis.

As the commission settled down to its task, Moses Olsen made one more demand. With the discoveries of Alaskan and Canadian oil assuming new importance following the quadrupling of world oil prices in 1973, he insisted that Home Rule should also incorporate recognition of the Inuit's original right to own Greenland's subsoil, and any mineral wealth it might contain. The Danes, like the Canadians, refused outright. If that was the Inuit's wish, the Danish Prime Minister warned, the Greenlanders would have to abandon their ties with Denmark.

Knowing this to be economically impossible, the Inuit compromised, accepting *fundamental* rights to mineral and oil resources, rather than the right of ownership. The Danes neglected to define the term, but the Inuit were reasonably happy, having won the right to veto any decision to extract resources.

After five years of discussion, the Greenlanders voted by 70 per cent to 26 per cent to adopt Home Rule. This was ratified soon afterwards by the *Folketing*. The 51,000 Greenlanders, of whom more than 9,000 are of Danish extraction, are now responsible for every aspect of home affairs, including education, employment, trade and industry, fishing, hunting, and country planning, as well as taxation, broadcasting, hospitals and the Church. The Danes, however, retain control of the foreign and defence policies, the police and the courts.

One of the first areas the Inuit tackled was education. Inuktitut immediately became the principal language in the schools, with Danish taught as a second language. Soon, approximately 12,000 children, more than a quarter of the Greenland-born population, were attending 100 schools, an average of 120 pupils to each school compared with 850 in Copenhagen.

Kayaker, Illulisaat, Greenland   *Author's photograph*

Traditional hunting and fishing methods were taught to ensure that the skills would not be lost, but these lessons were combined with classes on modern ecological and environmental theory so that natural resources would be farmed carefully. Many courses for further education were moved from Copenhagen to Greenland towns; training colleges for nursing, teaching, building, fisheries and sheep farming were established. (A tiny but important industry, with approximately 23,000 ewes in southern Greenland, sheep farming supports 500 people, including a hundred independent farmers; some 20,000 lambs are slaughtered annually.)

Shrimp processing factory, Nuuk, Greenland. Author's photograph

With international contacts between the Arctic nations increasing, the Greenlanders' progress was followed particularly closely in Canada and Samiland, where education, language and communications were vitally important in the battle to restore native pride. In Canada, the government had convinced most Inuit parents that unless their children were given an English-language education, they would be hard pressed to secure a decent future for them in the modern world. The awakening of Inuit political consciousness in the 1970s proved that this was far from true.

Demands for more lessons in Inuktitut and government support for Inuit teacher-training programmes quickly gained ground. The number of native students who continued their education after secondary school leapt from 16 to 154 in five years, and is still increasing. A one million dollar Indigenous Language Development Fund was established to help teachers design language courses and modernise Inuktitut. New words were invented to describe technological advances. The word for 'satellite', for example, became *qangattaqtitausimajug,* meaning 'it has been made to fly'.

When domestic communications satellites linked the Arctic to Canadian radio and television networks, the Inuit soon demanded their own

programmes.   *Satellite dish, Nuuk, Greenland.*

Author's photograph

Today, nearly half the output at the Canadian Broadcasting Corporation stations at Frobisher Bay and Rankin Inlet are in Inuktitut. Having learned the techniques of television, the Inuit formed their own broadcasting corporation, and were soon generating five hours of current affairs, cultural and sports programmes each week. Their ultimate ambition is to establish a circumpolar radio and television station which would beam programmes to Alaska and Greenland.

A constant theme in the Inuit programmes is the urgent need to protect the environment. This issue is so pervasive in the north that the Home Rule government in Greenland cited it as the principal reason for refusing to allow any form of offshore oil exploration in Greenlandic waters, although it agreed to drilling on land in eastern Greenland subject to stringent conditions. Reiterating that Greenlanders alone should own the country's natural resources, the new government signalled to the Danes that it would eventually wish to re-negotiate the terms of their agreement on mineral and oil resources.

The Greenlanders' immediate priority, however, was to extricate themselves from the then European Economic Community (EEC). When Denmark joined the market in 1973, the colony automatically became a member as well. To the Greenlanders, who hunted seals from kayaks and lived in a country which was ninety per cent ice, the rules and regulations of the bureaucrats in Brussels seemed irrelevant and absurd.

What was the purpose of common transport charges, they argued, when there were no roads, buses or trains, and the population of 50,000 was scattered in towns and settlements hundreds of miles apart? With almost no farming of their own, it would have been cheaper to buy agricultural products on the world market than be bound by the Community's Common Agricultural Policy. Similarly, the European Coal and Steel Union merely raised the prices for imported EEC steel to exorbitant levels.

The EEC (EU) is of little relevance to Inuit hunters
Author's photograph

In virtually every aspect, the wishes of the Inuit were at variance with EEC rules. The Community advocated free movement of labour between member countries. The Inuit were anxious to restrict the influx of foreign labour, especially from Denmark. The Common Market encouraged centralisation, the Greenlanders were eager to de-centralise. The European Atomic Energy Community, Euratom, stipulated that where extractable uranium existed, it should be mined to the advantage of its members. The Inuit, who were sitting on one of the largest uranium reserves in the world, refused because of the potential hazard to the environment.

The Inuits' greatest concern was the protection of the sea. Its teeming waters were their lifeblood, their only major resource. Yet the rules laid down by the policy-makers in Brussels were a strait-jacket. As long as the Greenlanders remained members of the Community, they could never be granted exclusive fishing rights in their own waters. To their annoyance, the catches of EEC (now EU) fishermen were worth five times as much as the subsidies they received from Community. 'It is intolerable', Moses Olsen told a conference in Denmark, 'to have to ask permission in Brussels to catch our own fish, especially as over and over again, we experience Community fishermen taking advantages in our waters beyond the granted quotas.

Community fishermen persistently caught more fish than they were allowed. As experience in the Arctic had shown so many times before, stocks inevitably declined. The depletion was so severe that reported catches dropped from 32,000 tons in 1971 to 6,000 tons four years later, but these figures were frequently manipulated. The International Council for the Exploration of the Sea reported that EEC fishermen sometimes took up to eight times the reported catch. Between 1977 and 1982, catches from east Greenland waters were logged at 50,000 tons, although 133,000 tons of fish were actually taken.

Marine biologists warned that the level of spawning stock was so low that the cod would stop reproducing off East Greenland unless catches were urgently reduced, but fishing continued unabated. The Greenlanders pointed to the West Germans as the only EEC nation with a deep-sea fleet large enough for exploitation on such a scale. They were equally angry at the EEC administrators, who in 1982 ignored a recommended maximum allowable catch of 62,000 tons in Greenlandic waters, and set the limit at 75,000 tons.

When the scientists urged a reduction to 56,000 tons the following year, the EEC maintained the quota at the same level, but by now, the Greenlanders had had enough. In a special referendum, the Inuit voted by 52 per cent to 46 per cent to leave the Community, with spoiled or blank votes accounting for the other two per cent. The turn-out was 75 per cent of the 32,385 people entitled to vote.

Negotiations for withdrawal were long and difficult. West Germany warned that it would exact a high price for the Greenlanders' departure. Not to be trifled with, the Inuit drove their own hard bargain. In return for allowing Community fishermen to take 68,000 tons of fish a year from their waters, they demanded an annual payment of £16 million, and won the status of an overseas associated country, which meant that they could sell their own fish on the European market without being tied by EEC (EU) red tape.

Until the last moment, like children squabbling over a box of chocolates, the ten member nations quarrelled about the terms of the withdrawal, and how the proportions of cod quotas should be shared. The date set for Greenland's departure was January 1st, 1985. In a last minute protest, the French petulantly exercised their veto, claiming that a special arrangement for Greenland could create difficulties in the Pacific, where the inhabitants of

New Caledonia were rebelling against French colonial rule. This extraordinary decision was followed by another bizarre incident when, despite repeated reminders, the Irish parliament 'forgot' to give formal approval to the agreement before the Christmas holidays. As a result, Greenland's withdrawal was delayed by one month.

Exasperation turned to anger. Jonathan Motzfeldt, the genial Lutheran clergyman who had become Greenland's Prime Minister, issued a stern warning. If by the end of the month the Community did not formally approve the terms agreed and pay the first cash payment, due on New Year's Day, he would call on the Danish navy to repel EEC fishermen from Greenlandic waters. Failing that, he added ominously, he would make alternative arrangements with the Soviet Union. Within 24 hours, the difficulties had been smoothed away, and on February 1st, 1985, Greenland became the first nation to leave the European Economic Community.

Although eager to maintain contact with Europe, the Greenlanders had always considered themselves an arctic, rather than a European, people. Their history, culture and temperament bound them to Alaska and Canada with whom they shared a common environment and similar aims. Not surprisingly, as the Inuit in the three countries engaged in their separate struggles, the bonds between them strengthened.

In July, 1977, hunters and community leaders from every part of Greenland converged on Sondre Stromfjord, an American air base on the west coast, where a chartered French-Canadian Boeing 737 was waiting to fly them across Davis Strait. After a brief flight to Frobisher Bay on Baffin Island, they were joined by a group of Canadian Inuit, each of whom had travelled separately from Labrador, Quebec, Baffin Island and Keewatin on the northwestern edge of Hudson Bay.

Taking off again, the Boeing, its bright blue fuselage gleaming in the summer sunlight, headed across Hudson Bay and over the Dene Nation. Somewhere ahead, a chartered Twin Otter packed with Inuit from villages and settlements in the western Arctic was flying along the same route, northwest along the Mackenzie River and across north Yukon towards Alaska. Their destination was Barrow, the northernmost tip of the North American continent. Here, for the first time in their history, one of the oldest races in the world met together as one people.

On arrival, the Greenlanders were elated to discover that although 3,000 miles separated them from the Alaskans, with whom they had virtually lost contact for 4,000 years, they had no difficulty talking to the Inuit of Barrow. Elsewhere, the centuries had left their mark, and the various groups were able to communicate with each other only when they spoke very slowly. Nevertheless, their common tongue was Inuktitut, and this was the official language at the meeting.

The Inuit resolved to call the assembly the Inuit Circumpolar Conference (ICC). They proposed a charter which would preserve their language and culture, improve transportation and communications, and safeguard Inuit resources. It would include scientific game management and the improvement of living conditions in the north. Formally constituting the ICC, the charter was adopted unanimously. The delegates shook hands, hugged each other and then burst into song. After centuries of isolation, the Inuit had become a united political force.

T   hey lost no time in settling down to work. Every aspect of arctic life was discussed: language, education and health care, land ownership, conservation and the encroachment of southern development. One of the most significant resolutions was that of an arctic peace zone, in which nuclear weapons, weapons testing, military bases and manoeuvres would be prohibited, together with the disposal of chemical, biological and nuclear waste. After vigorous debate, this proposal was adopted by an overwhelming majority.

Throughout the conference, the first concern of the delegates was to preserve the equilibrium of the arctic environment. In 1980, when they met again at Nuuk, the Inuit were horrified to learn of a Canadian plan to ship huge quantities of highly explosive liquefied natural gas in two super tankers from the High Arctic to southeastern Canada. Each ship would be more than a quarter of a mile long, with a beam the width of an ice-hockey rink. Fitted with 150,000 hp engines, they would smash through ice seven feet thick. No mention was made of the pressure ridges, which could be as much as 60 feet thick.

The plan, called the Arctic Pilot Project (APP), anticipated that on every voyage each vessel would carry approximately 140,000 cubic metres of liquefied natural gas, more than Greenland used in a year. The shuttle service involved sixteen round trips a year through the ice fields of the Northwest Passage, Baffin Bay and Davis Strait, a total of 64 voyages within 100 miles of the west Greenland coast. Financing the project were four major companies, including Canada's state-owned national oil and gas company, Petro Canada, and Dome Petroleum. With huge financial investments at stake, a titanic struggle looked inevitable.

The Inuits' main objection to the project was the danger to marine life. Experts called to public hearings before the National Energy Board in Ottawa testified that the noise from the powerful engines of the gas carriers, the largest ships in the world, would disrupt the sonar communication system of whales, and endanger their survival. There would be equally damning evidence from Greenlandic hunters. Attempts by APP executives to prevent them giving evidence were blocked by the Board, which ruled that their testimony was relevant and could be heard before the Canadian lawyer in the magistrates' court at Nuuk.

The first witness was Uusaqqaq Qujaakitsoq, a seal hunter and deputy mayor of Qaanaaq, the home of the Polar Inuit, who live further north than any other population on earth. He explained that when a police vessel sailed into Inglefield Bay during the beluga hunting season in 1979, the whales disappeared for the rest of the season. Similarly, when Inuit at Siorapaluk obtained snowmobiles, there was a marked decline in the number of seals in the district. The local council was so concerned, he added, that it had been forced to ban the use of snowmobiles for all but the summer months, when the seals retreat to the open water.

Pavia Nielsen, a hunter and fisherman from Uummannaq, described the difficulties encountered by hunters attempting to catch sea mammals. "In my own experience of hunting in kayaks, I know that the only reason I can get near the animals is because the kayak is silent," he began. "As soon as I make any noise, the animals disappear. I recall hunters who were approaching a narwhal, and knocked the side of their kayak with their paddle. As soon as that happened, the narwhal became alarmed by the noise and swam away."

The problem, Nielsen explained, was that when one seal, narwhal or whale was alarmed, it communicated with the others, and within a few minutes the fjord would be empty. The animals, he continued, were also sensitive to noise from ships.

"In 1975, when the Greenex company [a Danish subsidiary 100% owned by Vestgron Mines Ltd, which is in turn 62.5 % owned by the Canadian Corporation, Cominco Ltd.] began to mine zinc near Uummannaq, it sailed icebreakers through one of our good hunting areas. As a result, the animals went away from that area and the hunters had to hunt elsewhere. The whole fjord was affected for several months, until the community protested and put a stop to these icebreaking ships. There are now no icebreakers there, and so the animals have returned and we can hunt.

"If the APP goes ahead, we are afraid our entire way of life as hunters and fishermen will be completely destroyed. Furthermore, the APP is very dangerous because as a pilot project it will inevitably lead to other projects, and increased shipping in the area. This is what frightens us most."

With three-quarters of the Greenland population dependent on hunting and fishing for their subsistence, the Home Rule government was unanimous in its condemnation of the project. Greenland's representative in the European Parliament, Finn Lynge, wondered whether the Canadians realised the extent of the threat, and if they did, whether they cared. Fearful that the pilot project would lead to several supertankers a day breaking up the ice on a year round basis, his message to the Canadians was clear:

> "You simply cannot gamble in this way with the major livelihood of the majority of our population. Unless it is proven beyond a doubt that there is no danger at all, then the APP is unacceptable.
>
> "We are extremely concerned that the APP will break up the ice of the Lancaster Sound, which is the biological basis of life in Baffin Bay and Davis Strait, and disrupt the ecological food chains there.
>
> "We have some of the world's finest shrimp banks in Davis Strait. If there was a major supertanker accident, it would destroy these shrimp beds, and the entire industry.
>
> "Even if all the game does not go away, there is a grave danger that the stocks will be diminished to such a degree that we may have to depopulate vast areas of our country".

Clearly, the Canadians had given no thought to such dangers. Six months after the hearings began, the Arctic Pilot Project was shelved indefinitely. The decision was hailed as victory for circumpolar cooperation. In ten years, the Inuit had fought back from a position of isolation, helplessness and despair, and won back their pride. More importantly, they had gained the increasing respect of the *qallunaat* in the south as tough negotiators genuinely intent on preserving their way of life. In the years to come, they would need all the influence and stamina they could muster to combat the new, and infinitely greater dangers looming on the arctic horizon.

CHAPTER 3

The Wilderness Polluted

When hurricane force winds swept across the Kola Peninsula in the Soviet Union in 1983, the clear blue skies of the glorious arctic summer darkened without warning into a polar nightmare. For two days, clouds of stinging black dust blotted out the sun. In the city of Apatity on the shores of Lake Imandra, approximately eighty miles from the Finnish border, pedestrians were forced to protect their faces with handkerchiefs, hats, scarves and newspapers - anything they could find to avoid choking. Windows in every building remained firmly shut. Engineers switched off the ventilation plants in apartment blocks. Not until the gales had died down and the tiny particles of industrial waste had settled, did the people venture outdoors again.

The phenomenon was not unexpected. For years, officials had been discussing what to do with the industrial waste on the outskirts of the city. Over the years, the dumps had grown to 300 million tons, covering 1,375 acres. Each year, ten per cent of the waste from the ore-processing plant nearby was pumped into Lake Imandra. Another ten per cent was carried by the winds into the atmosphere. Samples of soil analysed by Soviet scientists showed that the thin layer of earth above the permafrost in this part of the Kola Peninsula was not only contaminated, bu't becoming saturated with chemicals.

In the industrial heartland of the Soviet north, massive quantities of sulphur dioxide, carbon monoxide, nitric oxides and other harmful substances are expelled from thousands of factory chimneys into the atmosphere. Pollutants from non-ferrous metal industries, which treat on!y one third of their harmful emissions, have been found in soil fifty miles away.

oviet executives in the metallurgy and mineral fertiliser industries of
S Murmansk province have been publicly castigated for showing too little
concern for the environment. Some factory managements have been
fined millions of roubles.So grave was the level of pollution that in one
seven-year period, 30,000 acres of forest were laid waste, much of it part of a
nature conservancy area in Soviet Samiland. Another 180,000 acres were
poisoned to such a degree that they may never be saved. Fortunatley,after
decades of careful work by scientists, the water of, and area around, Lake
Imandra is beginning to improve.

With its economy based primarily on steel production and the use of coal,
the Soviet Union is generally regarded as the principal source of pollution in
the Arctic, closely followed by West Germany and the United Kingdom.
Although the air in the Polar Regions is commonly believed to be the cleanest
in the world, recent studies show that it contains as many impurities as in
some suburban areas in the south.

For years, the Inuit have been puzzled by the gradual whitening of
traditionally deep blue skies. Now, scientists have identified the phenomenon
as 'Arctic haze'. Hanging listlessly over millions of square miles of the Arctic,
in layers as high as 25,000 feet, it is laden with sulphates and hydrocarbons
from coal, oil and petroleum products, and a chemical, perchloreothylene,
often used in dry-cleaning solutions.

The amount of chemicals in the polar air can be gauged by comparing hair
samples taken from modern Greenlanders with those from the bodies of a
group of Inuit found remarkably well preserved in a grave at Qilakitsoq, in
northwest Greenland. Carbon dating established that the Inuit had lived more
than 500 years ago, long before industrial pollution. Analysis showed that the
present-day Inuit were carrying significant quantities of cadmium, a metal
unknown when the Inuit family was alive in 1450.

The level of mercury, which has always been prevalent in the Arctic, is
300 per cent greater in today's Inuit, the copper content is 350 per cent
higher, and lead shows an increase of 700 per cent. The researchers warned
that a continued increase of poisonous metals in the atmosphere, combined
with the lack of important nutrients in some western food, would eventually
result in the diminished health of Greenland's population.

First noticed by pilots in the 1950s, Arctic haze extends from Norway to
the North Slope of Alaska. Scientists flying into it found that it was reddish-

brown, and much heavier and denser than at first believed. The pollutants are extremely acidic, and most noticeable during winter, when there is little rain or snow to wash them from the air. As a result, they remain airborne for longer and travel further. Now, the atmosphere is contaminated all the way to the North Pole.

The soot particles absorb the sun's radiation, give of heat and raise the temperature of the lower atmosphere. Many scientists believe that the haze traps this excess warmth, creating a greenhouse effect. Computer predictions indicate that if the pollution continues unchecked, weather patterns across the northern hemisphere could be distorted. Natural vegetation and crop patterns would change.

The icecap would begin to melt, raising the level of the oceans. Ultimately, many ports and low-lying coastal areas could be flooded. If this scenario seems far-fetched, it should be remembered that carbon dioxide levels in the atmosphere are increasing at the rate of one per cent a year, and that industry in the Soviet bloc, western Europe and North America discharges approximately 100 million *tons* of sulphur dioxide every year.

T   he enormity of this is difficult to grasp. By comparison, emissions of sulphur dioxide from Mount St Helens in 1980 and 1981 totalled only 300,000 tons. Expressed even more starkly, 100 million tons is equivalent to every single man, woman and child in the Soviet Union, East and West Europe, Scandinavia, Canada and the United States throwing a two-pound (one-kilogram) bag of sulphur dioxide into the air every day of their lives.

In addition to sulphur dioxide emissions, tens of millions of tons of nitric oxides and trace gases, many used in refrigeration and aerosol propellants, are discharged into the atmosphere. Recent studies show that if the emissions continue at their present level, the temperature of the atmosphere will rise as much as five degrees e. by the year 2050.

As the winds carrying these pollutants do not recognise boundaries, friction is created between nations. The Scandinavians are incensed because poisonous waste from Britain is affecting their forests and lakes, but Britain refuses to join formal international efforts to reduce the emissions. Canada and the United States are similarly at loggerheads.

When, in Helsinki in July 1985, ministers from nineteen countries signed a protocol to reduce sulphur dioxide emission by thirty per cent by 1993, Britain - which releases 3.5 million tons a year - refused to sign the document on the grounds that the percentage was arbitrary, and that in the 1980s it had cut emissions by 24 per cent. This compares with 37 per cent for France, 19 per cent for Italy and six per cent for West Germany. The average reduction for EEC countries is only seven per cent.

American researchers calculate that seventy per cent of airborne pollution in the Arctic emanates from Europe and the Soviet Union. This cannot be confirmed because Moscow has refused to cooperate with the study. Although some Soviet scientists have expressed concern that higher carbon dioxide levels may be melting the permafrost in Siberia, others apparently do not subscribe to the greenhouse theory, but suggest that the Arctic is becoming cooler rather than warmer.

Pointing to a marked increase of approximately 250,000 square miles in the amount of sea ice between Greenland and eastern Siberia, they say the mean temperature in some areas of the Soviet Arctic has fallen by 3°e. To some extent, this is borne out by the unusually severe ice conditions which have prevented Greenland's trawlermen reaching their fishing grounds. It is also supported by scientific projections of a new mini-glaciation period, based on the ice cores extracted from the Greenland icecap, and a thirty-day reduction in the time during which shipping can penetrate Soviet arctic sea routes.

A cause of equal concern in the West has been a £10 billion Soviet plan to reverse the northerly flow of the Irtysh and Ob Rivers, which feed the Arctic Ocean with fresh water, diverting them so that they run southwards through a I,500-mile canal to irrigate dry but densely populated desert zones. Advocates of the scheme dismiss arguments that the climate in the northern hemisphere could be adversely affected, although the effects cannot be established with certainty until after the event. The Soviet leader, Mikhail Gorbachev, has since indicated that he considers the scheme too grandiose, and may not permit it to go ahead. Rivers have already been polluted by industry throughout the Soviet Arctic, Samiland, and the North American sub-arctic regions. The water in Norway's River Tana is unfit to drink. Elsewhere, millions of salmon and trout have been killed.

In Quebec, excess water at a hydro-electric plant spilled into a swollen river, drowning thousands of migrating caribou. The animals, a prime source of meat for the Inuit, belonged to the 300,000-strong George River herd. Ranging across Quebec, the caribou migrate from the barren lands of Labrador, across the George and Caniapiscau Rivers, to the forests on the banks of Hudson Bay, a route they have taken for centuries. Fording the rivers is risky. Each year fast currents claim the lives of between 200 and 300 animals.

In September, 1984, torrential rains transformed the Caniapiscau River into a foaming torrent. Although the water level was twice as high as usual, the caribou plunged into the surging rapids as they had always done, driven by the need to reach their winter feeding grounds. So great was the force and weight of the current, that the hapless animals were swept downstream in a churning mass of bodies to Limestone Falls. There were few survivors. The carcasses were strewn along a thirty-mile stretch of river, heaped six deep along the bends, creating a major pollution threat to aquatic life, fish and game.

Altogether, 9,600 animals died. The Department of the Environment called in a fleet of helicopters to remove the rotting corpses. Fearful that another heard of 3,000 caribou heading in the same direction would meet the same fate, the Quebec Transport Department attempted to divert them by ordering aircraft to bomb the animals with water. As the extent of the calamity become known, the Inuit accused Quebec's power authority, Hydro-Quebec, and the James Bay Energy Corporation of causing the disaster. The Inuit alleged that the power authorities had allowed massive amounts of surplus water to flow into the river from the floodgates of a dam which was part of the James Bay hydro-electric project. The charge was denied vigorously. Hydro-Quebec officials answered that there had been twice as much rain as normally recorded for September, and declared the drowning to be an Act of God.

Subsequent investigation, however, disclosed that after the heavy rain, nearly 2,000 cubic yards of surplus water a second were released from the reservoir directly into the Caniapiscau River, more than doubling the flow. This appeared to be preferable to generating excess electricity that could not be sold, or to bypassing the turbines along a spillway into James Bay.

The decision was taken despite specific assurances, given when the Cree and Inuit signed the James Bay Agreement, that excess water would be released into the river only in an emergency, an assurance which, since completion of the reservoir in 1981, has been breached on many occasions.

Reports that the floodgates were first opened on September 4th made a nonsense of Hydro-Quebec's claim that the high level of water was due to heavy rain, which fell later in the month. Twenty-one days later, on the 25th, the Inuit appealed to the power board to reduce the spillage. As they did so, the caribou plunged into the water.

The volume of water gushing down Limestone Falls that day was nearly 3,700 cubic yards a second, more than half of it from the reservoir upstream. Four days later, or two days after the full extent of the calamity was realised, the flow rate was cut back to 1,300 cubic yards. A Canadian government report five months after the tragedy stated that human error was not to blame, and a provincial official claimed that caribou were frequently attracted to waterfalls because they sounded like a herd on the run.

Hundreds more caribou, the victims of traffic and hunters, were killed the previous winter after migrating too close to a temporary ice road, which had been built to service an isolated Canadian mine. Indeed, the construction of roads presents a serious threat to the people and wildlife of the tundras and barren lands. In Scandinavia, Samiland is marketed by government tourist agencies as 'The Last Great Wilderness of Europe', but tourists must have roads to reach the wilderness. Their arrival inevitably brings noise and disruption, and soon the wilderness is no more.

In Canada, roads built to supply pumping stations along the oil and gas pipelines to the north carry a steady stream of haulage trucks, security patrols and personnel. When the roads are opened to the public, there is an immediate demand for refuelling stations, fast food restaurants, hotels and lodges. For all of them, the greatest problem is getting rid of rubbish and sewage.

Before the *qallunaat* conquered the Arctic, waste was unknown. The few remnants of an animal's carcass left by Inuit hunters were eaten by other predators. Remaining food scraps were taken by arctic foxes, human excrement by the sledge dogs. Nothing was discarded. By contrast, in every village and settlement north of the tree line, the imported lifestyle from the south has left a trail of tin cans, abandoned vehicles, fuel drums, plastics, packaging and polythene bags. Attempts are made to burn the rubbish, but this is not possible with glass, metals and some of the plastics.

In the north, a little pollution goes a long way. Bin liners snatched by high winds from arctic rubbish dumps can be found hundreds of miles from the nearest settlement. The dry atmosphere preserves everything. On countless beaches, tin cans and old barrels from the stores of whaling ships wrecked in the 1840s can still be found. A chocolate bar paper wrapper, which could be expected to disintegrate within a year in a southerly climate, might still be blowing about the Arctic twenty years later. A plastic toy carelessly lost could provide a source of amusement to an Inuit child in 500 years time.

Grave, Resolute Bay. Author's photograph

Attempts to bury waste are usually frustrated by the lack of soil. In the far north, Nature takes 2,000 years to break down the sedimentary rock and create one foot of earth. In Greenland, Inuit in some of the coastal towns must bury their dead in graves hewn from solid granite. In areas where the permafrost is covered with only a thin layer of fragmented rock, the spring thaw forces the coffins back to the surface, so that the dead must be frequently re-buried or covered with a slab of concrete.

Evidence of pollution can be found in every village. Pepsi, Coke and beer cans litter the streets. Mounting piles of junk blight the exterior of virtually every home in the Arctic. Soggy packaging and insulation materials lie like mounds of rotting whale blubber a few feet from the front steps.

In Grise Fiord, on Ellesmere Island, the discarded head of a musk ox, perched on an old box, looks down on a scene familiar throughout the Arctic, a tangle of old metal- the rusting frames of beach buggies, snowmobiles, washing machines, refrigerators, freezers - the latter being visible evidence that the ice-cream salesmen from the south really *have* conquered the Arctic.

Descending to the road, frozen rivers of dish water make walking almost impossible. Sometimes, though less frequently now, black polythene bags tied carefully by the necks are stacked against the wooden houses, and await collection by council workmen. Known as 'honey bags', they line the pails gracing the corner of most bathrooms, and are filled with frozen household sewage.

"Honey" bags, near Resolute Bay, Lancaster Sound. Author's photograph.

Eventually, 'honey bags' are taken to a dump on the outskirts of the village. Here, they may be torn open by an arctic fox, polar bear or sledge dog on the loose. In low temperatures, the brittle polythene splits easily. When the temperature rises above freezing in early summer, the contents of winter ooze slowly into the sea. Similarly, the melting snow reveals the accumulated dog droppings deposited during eight months of polar darkness. In the meantime, the lethal rinks of frozen dish and bath water melt to form stagnant pools covered with the scum of detergents.

In Greenland, sewage disposal is more efficient, although the cost of installation and maintenance is frequently higher than the price of the house itself. The waste is carried along a network of pipes housed in insulated wooden tunnels which, raised above ground level, zigzag through the town to the local treatment plant. The sewage is prevented from freezing by a second pipe, carrying hot water for central heating. In smaller towns it is dumped directly into the sea.

The sea was also the recipient of effluent from the Black Angel lead and zinc mine run by the Danish company, Greenex A/S, at Marmorilik, in northwest Greenland. Concentrations of dissolved metals in Marmorilik fjord rose to such worrying levels that the Danish government ordered the company to examine alternative methods for the disposal of its tailings. The Greenland Fisheries Research Department found a marked increase in the lead and cadmium content in shrimps, seaweed, some whole fish and fish livers. The company made serious efforts to cleanse the effluent, with measurable success, but the amount of lead in mussels was later found to be unacceptable, and a ban was imposed on mussel harvesting within twenty miles of the mine. The mine is now exhausted and closed.

The threat posed to the Arctic by pollution, trade, shipping and industry is incalculable. The region is protected by fewer international conservation agreements than Antarctica, which, although similarly threatened, has no indigenous population. The Arctic Ocean, the fourth largest ocean in the world, acts as a thermostat controlling the temperature of the atmosphere.

Reflecting seventy per cent of the sun's rays back into space, the icepack ensures that the waters of the ocean do not become too warm in summer, and prevents the sea warming the atmosphere in winter.

Apart from a few restricted openings, such as the Bering Strait, this huge landlocked sea, like the Mediterranean, has only one entrance deep enough to permit a sufficient circulation of water. The passage lies between Svalbard and Greenland, and allows the warm waters of the Atlantic to flow northwards into the Arctic Ocean, while drifting ice and cold water are expelled back into the Atlantic.

The dual flow system keeps the water of the Arctic and Atlantic Oceans at a steady temperature, and is therefore of paramount importance for the weather system, dictating not only the climate in the United States, Canada, Greenland, Iceland, and Europe, but also the ecological chain in which polar cod is the key link.

If anything happened to the cod, which are very sensitive to temperature changes, there would be an immediate effect on the birds, seals, walrus, polar bears, foxes and every other species, including man. Yet, through this vital passage, the powerful flow of warm water carries with it not only oil spillage but millions of tons of chemical and industrial waste from western Europe and the eastern seaboard of north America. Once deposited in the ocean, the pollutants accumulate, trapped by the narrow exit.

A lthough strict international regulations have curtailed the deliberate pollution of the oceans, mariners secretly continue to flush out the tanks of their ships and dump oily bilge water at sea, rather than waste time and money in port. Tanker accidents are another major source of oil contamination. When the *Torrey Canyon* broke up off Britain in March, 1967, the oil spill affected 100 miles of British coastline, killed approximately 25,000 sea birds and severely disrupted marine ecology for a decade.

In February, 1970, nine million litres of bunker oil from the tanker *Arrow* covered nearly 200 miles of Nova Scotia coastline. The supertanker, *Amoco Cadiz*, which broke up off the Brittany coast in the spring of 1978, spewed 200 million litres of crude and bunker oil into the sea over more than two weeks. Like blackened chewing gum, the oil clung to 180 miles of coastline, and devastated the salt marshes which are essential to migrating birds. Some of the oil eventually drifted northwards with the currents into the Arctic

Ocean.

Anxious to ship oil from Prudhoe Bay and the Beaufort Sea through the Northwest Passage, the U.S. government in co-operation with the oil companies undertook an experimental voyage to test the feasibility of oil shipments in the rigorous conditions of massed icefloes. In 1969, the captain of the largest commercial ship flying the American flag, the 150,000-ton SS *Manhattan*, pointed its armoured prow north through Davis Strait and Baffin Bay, and headed for Lancaster Sound. As events turned out, it was fortunate that the supertanker, propelled by 43,000-hp turbines, was accompanied by icebreakers.

In the course of bearing down on one floe approximately a mile wide and nearly sixty feet thick, chunks of ice the size of railway carriages split off, screeched along the underside of the ship, and smashed into the propellers. The noise was so terrifying that the engine-room crew were said to have felt like deserting their posts.

Trapped by pack ice on several occasions, the *Manhattan* reversed and rammed the ice for up to twelve hours without making progress. Had the ship been carrying oil, there would have been considerable cause for alarm. Nevertheless, with the help of the icebreakers and helicopters, the supertanker did become the first commercial vessel to force a route through the Northwest Passage.

The Canadians had not been consulted about the voyage, and viewed it as a threat to the sovereignty they had unilaterally assumed over the Northwest Passage, waters which the Americans regarded as international. Shortly after the voyage, the Canadian parliament passed the Arctic Waters Pollution Prevention Act. Imposing strict security measures on ships sailing through the passage, it rendered their owners liable for compensation in the event of an accident. The Act also declared 'Canada's responsibility for the welfare of the Eskimo and the preservation of the very special ecological balance which exists today'.

A year later, in a speech in Toronto, Pierre Trudeau warned that the oil industry posed an incalculable threat to the Arctic. An accident would cause untold damage, he said, because oil spillage would not decompose in the cold climate, and for thousands of square miles would harm food sources for the Inuit and for wildlife.

Trudeau's concern, however, did not prevent his government from issuing exploration permits, nor restrain it from allowing Dome Petroleum to drill for four years before assessing the potential hazards to the environment. This was hardly surprising. As the largest shareholder in Panarctic Oil Ltd, a consortium of 37 companies, the government had a vested interest in the oil industry, and has repeatedly been accused of suppressing reports detailing the high risks of drilling in the Beaufort Sea.

While complaining bitterly about industrial pollution emanating from the United States, the Canadian government stubbornly refuses to act on environmental issues in the Arctic. Despite the urgent need for huge areas to be set aside to protect wildlife from pollution, Judge Thomas Berger's recommendation for a national wilderness park in north Yukon has still not been formally accepted.

Similarly, the Canadian government has ignored proposals for the International Biological Programme, which identified more than 151 specific areas in the Canadian Arctic as being crucial to wildlife and in need of preservation. In the entire Canadian Arctic, only one national wildlife area, Polar Bear Pass on Bathurst Island, has been established. After interminable investigation and discussion, the authorities finally decided to designate a second national wildlife park near Lake Hazen, on northern Ellesmere Island.

Similarly, when the Beaufort Environmental Assessment Review Panel, after three years of research and public meetings, recommended small-scale and phased development of arctic oil, the federal government chose to ignore the report. A member of a parliamentary standing committee on Indian Affairs and Northern Development, Keith Penner, admitted: 'If there is a big [oil] find, it will be hard to avoid megaprojects.'

The Canadian government's hunger for the profits from arctic oil apparently outweighs any desire to prevent an environmental disaster. The reason is clear: exploited fully, the vast reserves of oil and natural gas in the Beaufort Sea, estimated at four billion barrels and 300 trillion cubic feet, could revitalise the Canadian economy.

The dependence of the western world during the 1970s on potentially unstable Arab nations for its oil imports is another explanation for Canada's dismal environmental record. With price control and production rates dictated at the whim of Middle Eastern oil sheiks, the Americans and Canadians resolved to take steps to become more self-reliant. Together, they got through nearly seven billion barrels of oil a year, half of which was imported.

P roven reserves in Prudhoe Bay amounted to nearly ten billion barrels of oil and 25 trillion cubic feet of natural gas, making it the sixth largest oil field in the world. Panarctic, funded by the Canadian government, had drilled 173 wells at a cost of $750 million. It now expected to extract 2.5 billion barrels of oil in the coming decade. Suddenly, the ability to ship oil from the Arctic assumed new importance.

On February 6th, 1985, sixteen years after the pioneering voyage of *s.s. Manhattan*, Canada's Northern Affairs Minister, David Crombie, announced that the first crude oil would be shipped out of the High Arctic in September, 1985, when the winter ice was thickening. With the express permission of the Canadian cabinet, 100,000 barrels would be moved from Panartic Oil's Bent Horn field on Cameron Island, close to the Magnetic North Pole.

The ice-breaking bulk carrier assigned to the task was the *m. v. Arctic*, the heaviest vessel of its class in Canada. Improvements to the ship had cost the owners three million dollars, but at the time of the announcement it still failed to meet government standards for arctic shipping. Further modifications were undertaken to replace the bow and strengthen the hull. As work began, the federal government commissioned a $1.2 million study of High Arctic ice conditions, the first step in mapping a safe shipping lane for ships carrying oil through the harshest environment in the world.

CHAPTER 4

Black Ice

N otorious fluctuations in weather patterns and the unpredictability of the
ice present huge, perhaps unacceptable risks to shipowners contemplat-
ing regular oil shipments through the Arctic. Ice is a formidable enemy.
A floe can be five miles across with a keel as deep as a ten-storey office
block. Floating on currents, travelling between one and fifteen miles a day,
depending on the time of year, drifting pack ice can crush the armoured hull
of a ship as relentlessly as a steamroller squashes a seer can.

The danger is greatest during blizzards and fog. If a ship the size of s.s.
Manhattan, twice the size of the *Queen Elizabeth II,* can run into difficulties,
it is easy to imagine the hazards for smaller vessels. A margin of safety is
achieved only with the assistance of the most powerful icebreakers, but the
six ships of Canada's ice-breaking fleet are of insufficient tonnage to cope
with more than the three-month summer shipping season.

The older the ice, the harder is its consistency. Polar pack ice several years
old, crashing irresistibly into immovable shore-fast ice, creates what is
known as the shear zone. Creaking and grinding under the tremendous
pressure, chunks of cobalt-blue ice like boiled mints finally crack and break
off, refreezing in a chaotic jumble of pressure ridges. The resulting formation
of open water channels, *polynyas,* attract colonies of seals and thousands of
birds. Exposed to the colder air temperature, the surface water vaporises,
reducing visibility, and grounds ice-patrol aircraft. It is in precisely such a
hostile region that some of the oil men have elected to drill.

Drilling is usually conducted from ships or artificial islands. These,
instantly recognisable by their drilling towers and bright red hulls, are usually
protected by supply tugs which, with reinforced bows, push threatening
icefloes out of the way, not always a simple manoeuvre. A floe six feet deep,
a quarter of a mile in diameter and weighing more than two million tons takes
some stopping, even when moving at one mile an hour.

A momentum of five, or ten miles an hour, would pose a serious problem for the captain of a drillship. The process of abandoning a rig, and making sure that the well is safe, can take between eight and twelve hours. Yet, the decision to cut loose from the anchors holding his ship above the drillhole would have to be made quickly, and could cost his company more than a million pounds. So great are the dangers that the drilling season is restricted to three months a year. Ships are required to leave their drilling sites by early October. Then, the ice re-freezes so quickly that some captains, leaving their departure to the last minute, are lucky to make port without icebreaker assistance.

Artificial islands are safer, but not without problems. The earliest was created by cutting out of the ice a hole the size of two ice-hockey rinks. This was filled with sand and gravel, brought in by endless convoys of trucks along ice roads from the mainland. When the surrounding ice melted in the spring, the island remained. Known as sacrificial beach islands, they were built in less than 65 feet of water, and were protected from summer storms by sandbags. Their long, shelving beaches dissipate the energy of the waves. In winter, the ice broke up on the beaches, forming a barrier of protective rubble.

Arctic drilldrig.   *Imperial Oil*

When the oilmen needed to move into deeper waters, engineers designed a sturdier platform. Dredging an underwater hill from the sea bed, they filled with sand and gravel four concrete barges, or *caissons*, each weighing 5,300 tons, and sank them onto the summit of the hill. Locked together to form a square, the *caissons* acted as a perimeter reinforcement for the creation of the island, which was completed by pouring more sand and gravel into the hollow square. Later designs included artificial drilling islands linked by sub-sea pipelines to production atolls. These were large enough to accommodate four drilling rigs, oil storage facilities and a harbour from which ice-breaking tankers could ship the oil south.

Drilling is always risky. More than anywhere else, in the Arctic oilmen fear a blowout. This occurs when the subterranean pressure is so great that the mud in the drillpipe cannot contain the oil, gas or water being forced to the surface. When their instruments indicate a serious rise in pressure, engineers can seal the drillpipe with a preventer, but if friction from drilling melts the permafrost, the seal between the drillpipe and the frozen ground may be loosened, and leaks make the preventer useless.

An oil blowout in the arctic environment would be a catastrophe. Impossible to deal with in late August or September when the ice is forming, it would have to wait until the following May. During these nine months, a moderate blowout would spill approximately 500,000 barrels of oil into the sea. A severe blowout could release more than eight *million* barrels, contaminating the ice for hundreds of square miles, making oily pressure ridges in the shear zones. Chemical dispersal of that oil would not be practicable. The gushing well would blacken the underside of the continually moving ice, and oil spreading outwards from the well-head would broaden into a huge stain. Moving at three miles an hour, the discoloured ice would travel 840 miles in nine months.

In such a case the havoc to wildlife would be incalculable. The bird population in August is densest at the beginning of the drilling season. Approximately 100 species congregate in the deltas and open leads in readiness for their migration south. The Mackenzie Delta is particularly vulnerable. Oil drifting onto the mudflats and beaches would irreparably damage the feeding grounds for tens of millions of birds.

Great numbers of guillemots and auks would drown. These birds must leave the Arctic earlier than the other seabirds as their new feathers are insufficiently grown after the summer moult to enable them to fly by the time the ice re-forms. They swim instead, all the way from Lancaster Sound across Baffin Bay south to Greenland. Should they be caught in an oil slick, their oiled feathers would deprive them of insulation, and death would result from the cold or from drowning. A bird reaching land, in its attempts to preen the oil from its feathers, would probably die from asphyxiation or poisoning.

Equally appalling would be the effect on the marine food chain. During the first two weeks of summer, when the sun first appears above the horizon, the light seeping through the ice encourages the growth of plankton and krill, enough to feed every fish, bird and sea mammal throughout the season. An oil slick would annihilate this essential food source and lamentably affect the bowhead whales, beluga whales, narwhals, walrus, tens of thousands of seals, and millions of fish and crustaceans. Oil-covered seal would be inedible, and toxic to polar bears and arctic fox. The environment could take fifty years to recover.

R ecognising that a large oil spill over thousands of square miles would destroy the primary source of food for both the Inuit and the carnivores, in 1970 Pierre Trudeau said that 'the continued existence [of the Arctic] in unspoiled form is vital to all mankind.' Four years later, the Canadian government approved offshore drilling in the Beaufort Sea, fully aware that the oil companies did not have the capability for cleaning up a major oil spill. Evidently concerned about the risks, the government set up an organisation called the Arctic Marine Oil Spill Programme to investigate the problem. It concluded that the oil could be burned.

The inadequacy of such a plan became evident in 1979 when an offshore well poured 220,000 gallons of oil a day into the Gulf of Mexico. Every conceivable type of control, from booms to detergents, was tried with little success. Some of the oil was burned, but after five months the sea had been polluted with 82 million gallons of oil, the largest oil spill in history. The disaster highlighted the Canadian government's dilemma. If the oil companies could not contain the oil from a blowout in one of the world's most temperate climates, how could they hope to do so in the Arctic, during the months when the weather was at its most unpredictable?

Without answers, the Canadians pushed ahead with their master plan for dealing with an arctic spill. Hordes of bureaucrats would be galvanised into action, despatching teams of workers north to drill through the ice, and to ignite the oil bubbling to the surface. The heat would create basins into which more oil could ooze and be burned off, forming even larger basins. Squadrons of helicopters would drop firebombs onto the oil in a scenario that would do justice to a Hollywood farce.

No thought was given to the environmental consequences, although the nightmare effects of such a proposal are not difficult to imagine. For miles without number across the Arctic, thick columns of black smoke would rise into the atmosphere, eventually dumping the hydro-carbons onto the ice, into the sea or onto the tundra, polluting the plant life which plays as important a role on land as the plankton and krill in the sea.

The process would be repeated in the spring, when the single-year ice began to melt. Black oil attracting the heat of the sun would accelerate the melting process and lessen the time available for burning the oil before the ice became too thin to walk on.

The chances of complete success during such a cleaning operation are slender. The most optimistic assessment indicates that about 85 per cent of the oil could be burned off. The residue, like the ice trapped in multi-year ice, would have to be ignored. As it is thicker, this ice melts on the surface and freezes underneath. Oil trapped by the new layer of ice might not be released to the surface for a decade.

Officially, oil companies describe the chances of a blowout in the Arctic as minimal. Some tout odds of a million to one. Others, more realistically, put the chances at about one in 500. With arctic drilling carried out in areas of exceptionally high subterranean pressure, experts admit privately that if exploration and production continue unimpeded, an oil blowout is a statistical certainty.

Oil – and the Arctic unknown. Imperial Oil

The prognosis is based on the numerous gas and water blowouts that have already occurred in the Arctic. Dome Petroleum, drilling in the Beaufort Sea, has experienced water blowouts at three wells. In 1969, Panarctic was forced to remove a rig when hot water gushed out of the drillpipe to form a tower of ice hundreds of feet high. Shortly afterwards, another Panarctic project, at Drake Point on Melville Island, blew out of control after boring into a high-pressure gas deposit. Drilling engineers fought for two weeks to cap the well, which blew again a month later.

Despite heroic efforts, experts were unable to stem this second jet for a year, and nearly thirty million cubic metres of gas were lost. Within twelve months, a third Panarctic well, on King Christian Island near the Magnetic North Pole, caught fire. The 350-ft-high flame, the base of which was 100 feet above the gound, indicated the force of the jet. For three months, the fire burned nearly three million cubic metres of gas a day, and served as a beacon for pilots flying 100 miles away in the winter darkness.

Accidents are not as uncommon as one might imagine. Although offshore oil rigs are expected to withstand the 'hundred year storm', a severe arctic gale in September, 1985, forced Esso Resources (Canada) Limited to evacuate 87 men from Minuk I-53, an artificial island in the Beaufort Sea. They were just in time. Seven hours later, the rig, described by the company as one of its most modern, toppled over. Within a month, on the other side of the Atlantic, another eighty men had to be evacuated after a gas blowout ignited and killed a man on a Norwegian rig. Following a similar blowout less than a month later, tugs towed a second Norwegian rig away from a well operated by the same company, the government-owned Statoil.

Still haunted by the *Alexander Kjelland* disaster in March, 1980, when 123 men died in the North Sea after a leg snapped off and capsized the rig, Statoil immediately reviewed safety equipment and emergency procedures. The Norwegian Ministry of Justice appointed a special commission to report on the accidents. Trades Union leaders suggested that the Norwegian offshore oil industry was sacrificing safety for growth, a criticism which Statoil dismissed as nonsense, although it admitted that there could be no absolute guarantees against accidents in the oil industry.

Sounding remarkably like the Quebec- Hydro official who declared the deaths of nearly 10,000 caribou an Act of God, the company's spokesman claimed that the blowouts represented statistical averages, and suggested that 'it just happened to be our turn'. This nonchalant attitude was not reflected by the Norwegian Oil Directorate, which immediately reversed a previous decision to allow the first exploratory drilling in arctic waters during winter.

Oil companies have no specific code to follow in the event of a blowout. Each makes its own rules. These may be submitted to a government for approval, but governments seldom have personnel with sufficient technical knowledge to deal with highly complex problems, there are too few experts available to check too many procedures. As a result, safety precautions are sometimes waived, the rules bent to suit the circumstances. Although oil companies may establish strict rules, operators at the scene frequently ignore them. Spillage of more than five gallons, for example, should be reported to the authorities, but when approximately 1,500 gallons of P50 diesel oil overflowed from an experimental rig in the Beaufort Sea, no report was made.

Hundreds of similar incidents, including fires, go unreported. When one million gallons of diesel oil were accidentally spilled at Little Cornwallis Island, the Departments of the Environment, Northern Affairs, Fisheries and Oceans all failed to press charges. Despite warnings from federal officers, no action was taken. One oilman said: 'It was a perfect example of the government turning its back on environmental damage in the north. The oil industry is very skilful at playing off one department against another. The polluters are hardly ever punished. Only one or two cases a year are taken to court, although prosecution would have been warranted in a hundred cases.'

Despite the risks, the oil industry is set to transform the Arctic into a source of wealth greater than that in the Middle East. Expansion is planned on every front. Both Norway and the Soviet Union, the world's largest oil producer, are pushing the hunt for oil and natural gas north to Spitzbergen in the hostile waters of the Barents Sea, one of the stormiest seas in the world.

Here, the oil men have to contend with more than ice and storms. Frozen fog, sleet and rain cling to the exposed derricks. Radar masts, helicopter decks and the superstructure of oil rigs are equally vulnerable. Sea spray coats the bracings, moorings and chains of semi-submersible rigs. Intense cold reduces the efficiency of workers and freezes ballast water, fuels, fire fighting equipment and sewage systems.

Pushing the limits.   Imperial Oil

The effect of extremely low temperatures on drilling equipment is still not fully understood. Yet, with North Sea production expected to decline sharply early in the twenty-first century, the Norwegian government is committed to find new oil and gas wells to maintain output. Suddenly, Svalbard, the collective name for the islands around Spitzbergen, has sprung to prominence. Under the 1920 Treaty of Paris, 41 signatory nations have equal maritime, industrial, mining and commercial rights on the islands, subject to Norwegian law.

The Soviet state oil company, Trust Arktigkugol, has already begun exploratory drilling at Vassdalen, on the north side of Van Mijen Fjord in the Svalbard Islands, and a joint Norwegian-Swedish search for highquality gas is being intensified along the western edge of the islands. The chances of success are high. Soviet oilmen have discovered at least twenty new deposits of oil and gas in the Barents Sea, and are now operating their first semi-submersible rig off Kolgiyev Island. Although ships towing the rig to its position were delayed for several months by pack ice, the head of the arctic drilling operation, Ostap Sheremeta, was quoted as saying that he placed 'great stock in the reliability of the equipment and the eighty crew'.

The Norwegians are also operating a semi-submersible oil rig equipped with sophisticated data processing, said to be the first in the world which can operate round the year in the harsh arctic conditions. The Japanese manufacturer, Hitachi Shipbuilding, is renting the rig to Norsk Hydro, a government-financed concern which will now be able to drill to nearly 20,000 feet close to the North Pole.

If the oil companies strike lucky in Svalbard, which is 800 miles north of the Arctic Circle, they will be faced with the same nagging, and costly, problem as the Canadians: how best to transport the oil to refineries in the south. Norsk Hydro is planning to build a huge offshore factory in the Arctic Sea. Natural gas from production wells nearby would be converted to liquefied gas at a $5 billion terminal constructed on a concrete pillar attached to the sea bed. Shaped like a mushroom, the processing plant would be equipped with a sheltered harbour at its base, enabling liquefied natural gas (LNG) carriers to load the gas for export to Europe and the United States.

In Canada, serious consideration was given to a $6.1 billion pipeline, three and a half feet in diameter, from the High Arctic islands a few hundred miles from the North Pole to Ontario, a distance of 2,338 miles. The pipeline was to be buried in the permafrost, carry enough gas in a day to satisfy the whole of Canada and cross several sections of sea, one of them deep enough to cover a 68-storey skyscraper. Should such a pipeline rupture, engineers would be faced with enormous problems. If it was carrying oil, the damage would be inestimable.

Designers wrestling with the knotty problem of transporting oil and gas through the Arctic have produced a range of futuristic solutions. One proposal, from Boeing, called for a fleet of gigantic aircraft to load 1,000 tons of oil in special pods slung under the wings, each pod to be the size of a Boeing 747 jumbo jet. Flying twenty hours a day, these monsters of the sky would be powered by no fewer than twelve jet engines. In Japan, engineers are working on the prototype of a supership driven by electro-magnets. With no propellers, shafts or rudder, it would be capable of 100 knots on or underneath the sea, and result in a fifty per cent saving on fuel costs.

General Dynamics, the American company which builds Trident submarines and conventional gas tankers, put ten years' research into the development of a fleet of sixteen nuclear-powered cargo submarines. Each one would be capable of carrying more than a million barrels of oil from Prudhoe Bay, beneath the ice fields of the Northwest Passage, to the eastern ports of America. The oil companies, apparently wary of the horrendous potential for disaster, preferred to build the trans-Alaska pipeline.

After the first Arab oil embargo, the idea of nuclear cargo submarines was reviewed. New designs provided for the construction of submarine tankers the length of ten football fields, with a storage capacity of up to a million *tons* of oil. A study commissioned by the u.s. Department of Commerce concluded that such ships, costing $725 million each, were technically feasible and viable economically.

German designers preferred conventional submarines with strengthened hulls, towing a chain of clamp-on underwater barges. These, they claimed, would be particularly useful in *polynyas* and in the shallow waters of the Mackenzie Delta. Yet, apart from the effects on wildlife in the area, the underwater craft would be difficult to navigate in Davis Strait and other waters, in which icebergs as tall as electric power pylons have keels so deep that they frequently nudge the sea bed.

Oilmen tend to favour schemes above the surface. Dome Petroleum asked the world's foremost icebreaker experts from Finland to design a vessel that could operate in virtually any ice conditions. Having spent so much money on exploration in the Beaufort Sea that its $6 billion overdraft nearly wrecked the Canadian banking system, the company was anxious to solve the problem of transportation before the 1990s, when it hopes to start large-scale production. The Finns produced plans for a 150,000 horsepower tanker called an Arctic Marine Locomotive, which would be twice as powerful as the biggest icebreaker currently in service.

Despite these rapid developments, not even a nuclear icebreaker was able to help one of the ninety Soviet ships caught in sixty-foot-thick multi-year ice off the northeastern coast of Siberia in 1983. Among the trapped ships were smaller icebreakers which had been unable to force a channel for the other stranded vessels. Altogether, 26 ships found themselves in serious difficulty. Several were badly holed and in danger of sinking. When the ice cracked the hull and flooded the hold of the cargo ship *Nina Sagaidak,* the crew had to be rescued by the helicopter and flown to Vladivostock. The ship sank shortly afterwards.

Apart from the Finns, who have built sixty per cent of the world's icebreakers and operate its most advanced arctic research laboratory, the Soviets probably have a greater knowledge of arctic conditions than any other industrial nation. Their Finnish-built nuclear icebreakers are the most powerful on earth. The icebreakers of the future may keep arctic shipping lanes open, but accidents can, and do, happen. The danger is that as the icebreaking capacity increases, the temptation to extend the drilling season in the arctic oil fields will become irresistible.

CHAPTER 5

Untapped Treasure

Nuclear icebreaker   Author's

photograph

I cebreakers are the key to the exploitation of arctic riches. New discoveries of oil and gas off Svalbard, or in the Bering Sea, will increase the need for a regular icebreaking escort service for tankers and re-supply ships sailing between deep-water rigs, artificial islands and offshore factories. The huge mineral deposits in the North can be properly exploited only when icebreakers are able to keep regular shipping lanes open all the year. Without icebreakers, Canada's efforts to establish sovereignty over the arctic islands are little more than empty posturing.

The Canadian government, embarrassed by its inability to patrol for nine months of the year the icebound waters to which it lays claim, has ordered the construction of one of the most powerful icebreakers on earth. Due for completion in the 1990s, the $500 million 102,000 horsepower *Polar Eight* will operate in the Northwest Passage round the year, ploughing through eight feet of first-year ice at a steady three knots. With two-inch steel plates in the bow, it will be capable of ramming through sixty-foot thick ridges. In the words of one Cabinet document: 'The commitment of funds, construction and deployment of the *Polar Eight* will be a dramatic signal to Canadians and to the rest of the world that the government is serious about Canadian sovereignty in arctic waters.'

At the Arctic Research Centre in Helsinki, Finnish designers have proved that it is theoretically possible for ships of the future to smash through ice ridges measuring ninety feet from tip to keel, the equivalent of five London double-decker buses stacked one on top of the other. Arctic experts at Finland's Wartsila Shipyard anticipate the building of 210,000 horsepower icebreakers equipped with three rudders and three propellers, each thirty feet high with 70,000 shaft horsepower. The crucial difficulty is the $450 million price tag. Nevertheless, Wartsila engineers say there is now virtually no problem in the Arctic with which they cannot cope. Canada's *Polar Eight*, and a series of shallow-draught nuclear icebreakers being built by Finland for the Russians, are a strong indication of future developments.

Icebreakers have transformed Finland's own trading patterns. Until the 1970s, winter ice in the Gulf of Bothnia and the Baltic Sea closed the northern ports of Kemi, Qulu, Raahe and Vasa, denying Finnish industry access to the world's oceans. The only link across the Gulf was a temporary ice road from Vasa to Umea in Sweden. A decade of heavy investment not only gave the country an unrivalled lead in icebreaker technology, but enabled it to develop the paper, pulp, chemical and steel industries at its northern ports, which are now open every month of the year.

In the next decade, arctic shipping will flourish. The forward propellers on icebreakers will be replaced by air bubbling systems which reduce friction between the hull and the ice. Satellites in polar orbit will enable icebreaker captains to plot within a few feet the channels of least resistance. Air cushion vehicles, or hovercraft, with specially designed skirts for use in abrasive ice and low temperatures, will transport cargo and relief workers to offshore oil rigs, or skim over the permafrost and river estuaries of Siberia.

Russian designers have produced plans for an underwater icebreaker which might have been conceived by Jules Verne. With the body of the ship immediately beneath the surface, steel teeth along the top of the hull could cut through the ice as a diamond cuts glass. At the stern, the control tower and a helipad are perched on top of a sixty-foot wedge-shaped pylon, which would slice through the broken ice like a snowplough cutting through a snowdrift. The ship would submerge repeatedly if the ice was too thick and surface like a whale at play, smashing the underside of the ice with the upper, armoured part of its hull.

Each winter, Russian convoys in the Arctic Ocean push further east towards the Chukchi Peninsula, where the multi-year polar icepack extends almost to the shoreline. Despite the constant hazards, but aware for thirty years of the enormous potential of the Arctic, the Russians invested in their first atomic icebreaker, *Lenin*, which has since escorted ships for more than a million miles. Later additions to the nuclear fleet opened up year-round shipping lanes from Murmansk to the Yenisei River, along which hundreds of vessels annually move approximately five million tons of cargo.

Soon, a new generation of ships will be in service, shallow-draught icebreakers designed for use in river estuaries, a fleet of icebreaking cargo ships and huge nuclear tugs capable of towing more than seventy barges with a load of 1,300 containers. During the 1990s, the ancient dream of opening trade routes through the Northwest and Northeast Passages to China, Japan and Asia is almost certain to be fulfilled.

The untapped treasure of the North extends right across the Arctic. There are massive deposits of lead and zinc, copper, nickel, iron, manganese and uranium, and waiting to be mined a treasure store of platinum, gold, silver and diamonds. The North Slope of Alaska has reserves of 150 billion tons of coal, with eager buyers in Taiwan and Japan, which are approximately the same distance from Barrow as San Francisco. Until recently, these riches were inaccessible. Now, there is the manpower, the money and the means to extract and transport them to the South.

Siberia, 4,000 miles wide, stretching east from the Urals to the Pacific, is twice the area of the United States and contains half the earth's hydro-carbon reserves. There is enough coal to supply the world for 600 years. The region provides 65 per cent of the Russia's oil, 82 per cent of its natural gas, 30 per cent of its timber, paper and cardboard, 20 per cent of its electricity, and 73 per cent of its mineral resources. By comparison, mineral production from Canada's Northwest Territories is approximately eight per cent of the Canadian total. Russia will soon be the world's largest exporter of natural gas. More than 20,000 million cubic metres are transported annually along the world's longest trans-continental gas pipeline from Urengoi, in the far north, to western Europe, a distance of 2,700 miles.

Russian taiga, Sakha Republic. Agency

Huge supplies of natural gas in eastern Siberia and Yakutia, a province of the size of Portugal wedged between Siberia and the Russia Far East, are thought to exceed all those known in the Middle East. Eventually, Yakutian gas will be piped thousands of miles for export to Japan from a Pacific Ocean port still to be built.

Yakutia, the coldest region in the northern hemisphere with winter temperatures dropping to - 70°C. is so rich in mineral resources that according to local legend, when God flew over the region distributing riches over the earth, His hands froze and He dropped them all. These resources include the largest gold and platinum deposits on earth (the largest nugget found in Yakutia weighed approximately 21Ibs.), and diamond fields so large that Russia is now the second largest producer in the world after South Africa. Such wealth makes Siberia and Yakutia the mightiest industrial area of the future, with the potential to transform Russia into the world's richest country by the end of the century.

Largely ignored by the west, the taming of Siberia, Yakutia and the Russian Far East is a story of remarkable human achievement. No longer the preserve of hunters, trappers and reindeer breeders, these icy wastelands are the key to the future economic health of the nation. To supplement the countless citizens drafted into the mines for alleged infractions of the law, hundreds of thousands of workers are being enticed into mines, hydro-electric plants and industrial complexes, attracted by earnings two-and-a-half times the Russian average.

Siberian workers receive longer holidays and every third year a free return ticket to any destination in Russia. After fifteen years' arctic service, they are entitled to a full pension five years earlier than other employees (Russian men normally retire at sixty, women at fifty-five), an inducement which has helped to halve the number of families leaving the region, and encouraged immigrants to settle in the remotest towns. Some leading Russian economists, however, claim that the number of workers moving north is declining, and believe that new ways must be found to motivate potential migrants.

Apart from the climate, life in the Arctic is similar to that in other parts of Russia. When the former Canadian premier, Pierre Trudeau, visited Norilsk, a modern city close to the copper, nickel and,cobalt mines east of the Yenisei River, he described it as the eighth wonder of the world. Here, in temperatures well below the freezing point of mercury, the 270,000 metallurgists, miners, researchers, industrial workers and their families (who between 1974 and 1984 helped to double the city's population) enjoy all the amenities of other Russian towns.

Norilsk has nearly 2,000 apartment blocks, many of them thirteen storeys high, served by the city's own hydro-electric plant. There are colleges, secondary schools and nursery groups, hospitals, clinics and about 1,000 doctors. Each year, 3,000 couples get married and 4,000 children are born. For recreation, there are theatres, cinemas, libraries, a concert hall and an art gallery, and restaurants, cafes and bars. The city has forty streets, twelve supermarkets, hotels, and health centres with evergreen plants, aquariums and exotic birds from South America.

Throughout the winter, the inhabitants of Norilsk compete in gymnasiums at the Arktika Palace of Sports, which boasts several swimming pools, heated to 36°C. In good weather, thousands of people take part in ski races on illuminated courses through the surrounding tundra. Similar Siberian towns have built a total of approximately 9,000 gymnasiums, 400 stadiums and more than 100 swimming pools, many of them of Olympic standard.

Apartment blocks, Norilsk, Russia.
Russian Embassy

Apartment blocks in Siberia are built on beds of deep gravel or on piles, which allow cooling winds to blow freely underneath the buildings. As in Greenland, central-heating pipes are carried above ground in insulated ducts. Protection against storms is maximised by placing buildings close to each other in semi-circles. The areas between them have transparent roofs, beneath which there are winter gardens, children's playgrounds, fountains and tropical plants. The lower floors are reserved for public use to give the inhabitants covered access to schools, kindergartens, clinics, shops, cafes and other facilities. Town planners try to reduce the risk of frostbite out of doors by ensuring that the distance from anyone apartment to a bus stop is no more than 300 yards.

Fierce winds, freezing temperatures and the permafrost have forced Russian construction engineers to adopt new building techniques and planning concepts. In such extreme temperatures, drills snap, tools break, machinery breaks down, fuel freezes, rubber crumbles, synthetic materials split and concrete must be steam-heated before use. Permafrost creates special problems.

Poorly-designed houses built directly on the frozen ground generate too much warmth, melt the sub-surface ice and eventually disappear into holes of their own making. Similarly, a subterranean hot-water pipe not only melts the permafrost, but creates streams of melting water, which eut through the ice so rapidly that in a few months a pipe one foot in diameter could gouge a trench six feet deep and ten feet wide.

Driving across the Siberian tundra in winter
Russian Embassy

So sensitive is the arctic environment that the driver of a single vehicle crossing the frozen tundra could unwittingly leave behind a trail of swampy pits and craters hundreds of miles long. Churning up the thin layer of moss and lichen, the wheels can expose the soil beneath, which, unlike the ice which reflects the sun's rays back into the atmosphere, will attract its heat and melt the permafrost. Within weeks, the tracks will subside into wide, muddy channels, scars which could remain for decades.

This phenomenon is the principal reason for the lack of roads in the north. Foundations of rock or concrete, unavailable locally, must be five feet thick, making construction usually impracticable owing to high transportation costs. Some areas of permafrost have been damaged permanently, partly due to excessive timber felling. Russian scientists believe another reason may be the high concentrations of carbon dioxide in the atmosphere raising the temperature of the air close to the earth's surface. This is a matter of grave concern. Should the permafrost thaw on a large scale, the scientists believe there could be widespread disruption to roads, railways, building projects, and by implication, the entire future of the Russian economy.

Serious problems undoubtedly remain. The development of Siberia is dogged not only by the climate and terrain, but by bureaucracy and greed. The Communist party newspaper, *Pravda*, recently criticised factory managers in the central and southern regions for despatching shoddy and unrequested goods to Siberia and the Russian Far East, fully aware that it would not be possible to return them once the supply routes were closed. Some factories were allegedly despatching thousands of unordered women's coats and hats to the north.

'Generally speaking, these goods are old models and of poor quality,' *Pravda* noted. 'The managers do it to fulfil their production plans.' When local people attempted to return stock the following spring, the newspaper reported that officials in Moscow refused to supply them with containers, with the result that in some remote settlements the shops, filled with unsolicited and unsold goods, looked more like warehouses.

A survey by a leading sociologist at the Novosibirsk Economic Institute, home to some of the Russia's most radical official theorists, indicates that ninety per cent of the managers and eighty-four per cent of the workers believe changes in the centralised economy would increase local responsibilities and boost efficiency. Theorists suggest that the present system, which is dominated by ministries in Moscow, encourages laziness and indifference, the production of defective goods and the concealment of losses in production. Anxious to rejuvenate the economy, some Russian economists are now calling for younger, more dynamic management and business schools run on lines similar to those in the west.

Feeding Siberia's multiplying population is another nagging difficulty. Most of the land in the north is poorly drained. Soils are acidic and deficient in soluble plant foods. Crops can grow only in protected soil. Consequently, most of the 150 million acres of cultivated land are in southern Siberia where the average annual rainfall is low, and crops must rely on irrigation. With food-producing areas representing less than three per cent of Siberia's total acreage, approximately ninety-five per cent of its food must be obtained from other regions.

Reindeer herds are a useful supply of meat, although the lack of a comprehensive road network makes transportation slow and costly. There are some sheep and goats, but pigs, poultry and dairy animals are rare, and great distances prevent the regular distribution of milk, eggs and vegetables from the south. Yet, if the riches of Siberia and the Russian Far East are to be fully exploited and the region successfully populated, the provision of a reliable food source is of paramount importance. For this reason, the role of the agronomist has become crucial to Siberia's future.

At the Agricultural Research Centre near Novosibirsk, Siberia's largest city, researchers at ten institutes and eleven experimental farms are grappling with every aspect of arctic plant breeding, fertilisation, fodder and livestock farming. Their latest findings indicate that more than 330 million acres of new land can eventually be cultivated. Experimental fields in western Siberia are said to have produced high yields of cabbages, carrots and radishes. Agronomists have developed a new type of tomato, nicknamed 'Speedy' because of its rapid growth rate in northern latitudes. Land improvement is expected to provide extensive new acreage for potato and green vegetable crops.

In Yakutia, other seedlings raised under glass are reported to have produced yields per acre of up to sixteen tons for cucumbers, twenty tons for tomatoes and twenty-four tons for cabbages. During the brief summer, cabbages exposed to continual sunlight grew larger leaves than the same varieties in the south, a remarkable achievement in a country in which the winter temperature is so extreme that exhaled breath freezes instantly into a fog of minute, needle-sharp ice particles.

At Tomsk, in northwestern Siberia, a ninety-acre state farm feeds 500,000 people. Imported poultry and pigs provide a hundred million eggs and hundreds of tons of meat a year. This, however, is an exception. Although each town grows its own tomatoes, cucumbers, radishes, potatoes, cauliflowers, carrots and other root crops in extensive hotbeds and hothouses, farming in Siberia provides little more than five per cent of the region's food, and many more farms like the one in Tomsk are needed urgently.

Adapting hardy crops to the extreme climate is not the Russian authorities' only concern. Eventually, they hope to be able to control the weather, prevent the formation of ice and tap vast sources of energy from volcanic heat zones deep beneath the permafrost. Tens of thousands of experts at fifty research and design institutes are conducting an impressive array of scientific studies. These include research on mineral, forest and water resources, on health, and ecology and the effects of industrial complexes on permafrost. Under the auspices of the prestigious Academy of Sciences, the findings are pooled into the 'Siberia Programme', the nation's top-priority research project. Essential to the country's future economic health, its purpose is to transform the icy wastelands of Siberia into the key fuel and energy base for the whole of Russia.

Such importance is attached to Siberia that in recent years Russian authorities have channelled more than 10,000 students through the Arctic College in Leningrad into scientific research communities at Novosibirsk, Irkutsk, Yakutsk, Krasnoyarsk and Tomsk. The largest of these science cities is Akademgorodok, fifteen miles south of Novosibirsk, a city of more than a million people. Here, some of the best minds in the country, supported by 15,000 researchers, technicians and staff, are tackling the present and future problems of Siberia. Their efforts have already produced new welding techniques and fine-grained metals with a high degree of plasticity and greater resistance to extreme cold.

Russian scientists predict that in the future, plastics will play an increasingly important role in the Arctic, especially in housing. Premoulded walls, window and door frames will replace bricks and concrete, and improve insulation. Lightweight plastics will be easier and cheaper to transport, and mass production will reduce labour costs. In the opening decades of the twenty-first century, a major feature of the North will be the self-sufficient plastic towns covered by translucent domes, with a micro-climate supplied by natural gas. In other developments, new railways are being built and engineers are studying the feasibility of building roads supported by hopper-carrying girders. The piles would be used for supporting power lines, telephone cables, and possibly oil and gas pipelines.

B y reversing the flow of Siberian rivers, and by regulating and diverting them, another great source of power will be available. Dozens of hydro-electric plants are planned or under construction, each one the nucleus for a constellation of towns, mines and power-intensive industries. The mighty River Yenisei, nearly 2,000 miles long, is able to support power stations with an aggregate capacity of 70 million kilowatts. The twelve generators of the Krasnoyarsk station, until recently the largest in the world, produce six million kw, more than two and a half times the output of the Grand Coulee Dam, the largest plant in the United States. A second colossus on the Yenisei is producing 6.4 million kw. Similar projects are in progress on other rivers, notably the 1,200mile Kolyma River in the extreme north east of the country.

Water polluted by industry is a central anxiety. Icebound for as much as eight months a year, northern rivers receive too little sunlight, are low in oxygen content and easy to pollute. It is ten times more difficult to clean an arctic river, which must flow 1,250 miles to purify itself, than a temperate-zone river, which will cleanse itself in 125 miles. Russian authorities appear to be increasingly aware of the dangers. Although local managements are frequently insensitive to the environment, conservationists are gradually winning the battle to educate them, proving that a sound ecological approach can be beneficial.

The city of Norilsk, pride of the Russian Arctic, is a typical example. For years, the metal industry had contaminated the city air with sulphur dioxide, until researchers discovered that the gas could be trapped by an efficient filtering system, and converted into sulphuric acid which was in short supply. Gradually, a heightened awareness of the environmental effects of industrial projects is permeating the bureaucracy. Permission to build hydro-electric plants is no longer automatic. A proposal for a massive power complex on the River Ob was recently defeated after scientists pointed out that the reservoir would attract heat from the sun, thaw out vast plains in the north and destroy the regional climate. The government accepted this view, and cancelled the project.

W   ith such an enormous demand for power, the advent of nuclear energy
        in the Arctic was inevitable. An atomic plant at Bilibino, hundreds
of miles north of the Arctic Circle in the hostile region near the East Siberian Sea, is the most northerly in the world. Nuclear power is being exported from a network of atomic plants on the Kola Peninsula. More atomic power stations are intended for northern Siberia. Determined to meet growing energy demands, Russian authorities are now planning the country's first tidal power plant, which will harness the waves along the coast of the Kola Peninsula. Three similar plants, with a total capacity of more than 100 million kilowatts, will be built on the shores of the Okhotsk Sea, in the Russian Far East.

The scale of development in Siberia during the past 35 years can be gauged by the growth of Bratsk, which in 1951 was a typical village of 4,000 people living in huts, tents and wooden cottages. Today, it is a bleak metropolis of approximately 300,000 people sprawled round a hydro-electric plant, which supplies timber processing factories, industrial complexes and an aluminium works, the annual output of which surpasses production for the whole of western Europe.

Moving goods and people across the vast distances of the Russian Arctic is a daunting task. Roads are almost non-existent. Siberia's only main highway, running between its largest cities, Yakutsk and Norilsk, is a nightmare. In summer, drivers motoring through dense clouds of mosquitoes are obliged to stop every few miles to clean windscreens blackened by tiny corpses. Autumn and winter blizzards bring convoys to a halt. Frost breaks up the surface. Other routes are not roads at all, but unmarked, seasonal tracks across frozen swamps or on river ice. Driving calls for expert map-reading, navigation and eyesight. In spring, patches of thin ice are a hazard, sometimes costing a driver his life, and at others forcing him to abandon his load until it can be retrieved by helicopters or by another truck.

Siberian rivers offer a more convenient method of transport. Each year, ships ferry hundreds of thousands of passengers and more than 100 million tons of freight along approximately 42,000 miles of navigable waterways. Unfortunately for Russian planners, most of these critical arteries, like the roads, are open only for a few months a year, and whereas the movement of passengers and freight tends to be in an east-west direction, the majority of rivers flow from south to north.

For many northern towns, the one lifeline is air travel. More than a third of all mail and cargo carried annually in the Russia is destined for Siberia and the Far East. At many smaller towns, pilots land on dirt runways or the ice. Unpredictable weather makes schedules uncertain. As in the west, the expression 'Hurry up and wait' applies. Frustrating though this may be, without regular flights passengers would need weeks to reach their destinations and business would come to a standstill.

Helicopters play an equally important role, delivering food and mail, evacuating the sick, ferrying equipment to mines and factories, and gas pipelines and rail tracks to isolated outposts.

Railways, which run south of the arctic zone, but provide essential staging posts for Siberian exports, are by far the most reliable form of transport. Until the 5, 778-mile Trans-Siberian railway was built in 1897, the sledge journey between Moscow and Vladivostok took nearly a year. Today, freight trains laden with food, clothing and machinery complete the run in seven days, returning with minerals, coal and timber. For European manufacturers, shipping goods to Leningrad, across Siberia by rail, and from the Russian Pacific coast by sea to Japan and Hong Kong can be twenty days faster and forty per cent cheaper than using traditional sea routes through the Suez and Panama canals.

Keenly aware of this, Russian authorities sanctioned a second major rail link to the Pacific, the Baikal-Amur Mainline railway, affectionately known as BAM. The 2,000 miles of double track, of enormous economic importance, runs 200 miles north of the old, over-burdened Trans-Siberian line, which was deemed to be too close to the Chinese border for the peace of mind of the defence strategists.

Opening up 600,000 square miles of virgin territory, BAM gives access to a treasure trove larger than the combined land mass of Britain, France and Italy. Rich in asbestos, salt, copper, gold and other precious metals, it contains 45 billion tons of coal, 21 billion tons of iron ore and more than half Russia's timber and fresh water resources.

H   ailed as the construction project of the century, BAM and its builders provided the national press with an abundance of statistics and innumerable stories of heroic Russian workers struggling against impossible odds to the greater glory of Socialism. Conditions for the 132,000strong workforce were indeed appalling. Lured to Siberia by pay packets as much as four times the national average and the promise of rising to the top of long waiting lists to buy a car, many workers and their families were forced to live in cramped, poorly-insulated railway carriages in temperatures below -50°C. Army engineers equipped with dynamite and flame throwers were repeatedly called in to force a route through deep snow and ice, blocks of which were sometimes 1,000 feet thick.

Working in atrocious weather, engineers laid two-thirds of the track on permafrost and forged a route through one of the world's worst earthquake zones, in which as many as 2,500 tremors are recorded each year. With some tremors registering between seven and eight on the Richter scale (the March 1960 earthquake at Agadir which killed twelve thousand measured 6.6) the ultimate frustration must have been having to tunnel eighteen miles through solid rock. One tunnel was nine miles long.

In another, the rock fractured twenty times in a 300-yard section, with some fissures thirty feet wide. Despite the difficulties, engineers pushed BAM across seven mountain ranges and built more than 2,000 bridges, of which 142 crossed fast-flowing rivers hundreds of yards across, an average of one bridge or tunnel for every mile of track.

After ten years' labour, the £5 billion railway was completed. Within months, construction began on a new line linking BAM to Yakutsk, 500 miles further north. The spur, due to be finished in 1995, will require 700 bridges. Seventy million cubic metres of earth must be transported to the track-laying site to make the foundations in the permafrost. Eventually, more than one million people are expected to settle in new towns along the railways, and a new industrial belt will be born.

Having invested £140 billion in Siberia since World War Two, Russian authorities intended to build more than 350 new towns, most of them with resident populations of up to 200,000 people. Siberia's current population of approximately 27 million was expected to swell to 100 million by the end of the century. By comparison, Canada's Northwest Territories, which are three times smaller, have a population of 50,000. There is little doubt that this imported population, if it materializes, will learn to survive the Siberian climate. The state of the Russian economy at the beginning of the 21st century, however, may cause all these plans to be abandoned – or at least shelved.

If they do go ahead, the effect on the native peoples of Siberia can only be detrimental. Concern for the ethnic minorities in Russia has always been minimal. Long before the 1917 Revolution, corrupt Tsarist officials introduced drunkenness and disease, and exploited Siberian natives by forcing them to pay a fur tribute, or tax. The Tsarists, however, made no attempt to educate them, improve their medical welfare or to interfere with the structure of the ethnic communities.

This was in contrast to the Bolsheviks, who regarded the Siberian natives as backward and in need of political enlightenment. In the course of providing this, they successfully eliminated much of their traditional way of life. In today's highly politicised one-party state, an influx of workers on the scale envisaged cannot help but have a damaging effect on the remaining traditions of such boreal ethnic groups as the Sami, Nenets, Nganasany and Dolgans, or in Siberia and the Russian Far East, the Yakut, Yukagirs, Eveny, Chukchi and Siberian Inuit. The real issue, however, is whether the Arctic itself can cope with such an onslaught.

CHAPTER 6

The Arctic Challenge

I n the scramble to unlock and protect the arctic treasure chest, the Inuit and the other natives of the Far North have been overwhelmed and forgotten. The attitudes of miners, oil men, politicians and military chiefs are in essence no different from those of the whalers and traders, or the explorers, missionaries and Danes. None of them intended to undermine the livelihoods of the happy and gifted peoples with whom they came into contact.

The brawling whalers, accustomed to the rough and tumble of shipboard life, are unlikely to have given a second thought to the effects of their violence on a peaceful society. The missionaries, impervious to all but the spread of Christianity, simply did not understand that female infanticide, suicide and the desertion of the old and sick were, if evil, a necessary evil for the survival of the group. The Danes were thoughtless in their dealings with the *qallunaat* have trickled through the Arctic, and worn away a culture.

The stream became a torrent with the construction of the DEW line in the 1950s. In a few short weeks, hunters accustomed to hoarding the smallest scraps of food saw more waste than they or their ancestors had known in 4,000 years. Uninvited and without warning, ships, helicopters and pot-bellied transport planes appeared over the horizon. In Greenland, to the amazement of the 118 descendants of Robert Peary's Inuit at Thule, the convoys and aircraft dumped hordes of fresh-faced men and countless tons of cargo barely a harpoon's cast from their traditional hunting grounds and houses of turf and stone.

Intrigued, excited and bewildered, the Inuit stood by their dog teams and watched the intruders drive heavy trucks and bulldozers down the ramps. Innumerable sheets of corrugated iron were unloaded. In a single day the strangers bolted them together to create a city of tunnel-shaped huts and hangars. Soon, soldiers had flattened a 10,000-foot runway along the valley. More aircraft circled overhead, and on landing disgorged drums of fuel and crates of food, which were stockpiled in the unloading bays, a store greater than the impoverished Inuit had seen, or heard of, in a lifetime.

White radar domes, like giant golf balls, took shape, followed by a radar scanner so huge that it was likened to a football pitch tipped on its side. Nearby, a communications mast only slightly shorter than the Empire State Building rose into the sky. Before the Inuit could discover what was happening, the listening post for Armageddon had been established.

In two years, 20,000 men passed through Thule, which grew into one of the biggest air bases in the world. The resident staff of 3,000 men carved tunnels in the ice, abandoned or burned trucks which failed to function in the cold and littered the landscape with discarded packets of chewing gum and Camel cigarettes. Heaps of uneaten food were left for the foxes. Whipped by the high winds, empty barrels of fuel trundled across the valley or out to sea. After a year, the Danish Minister for Greenland announced that the Inuit had voted to leave Thule for Qaanaaq, 100 miles further north. From that time on, the U.S. airbase and its environs were out of bounds.

Thirty-one years later, in 1985, the Greenland Home Rule government demanded from Washington between three and five million dollars, compensation with which to support the hunters Peary had called 'my eskimos', and replace the 27 poorly-insulated, one-room wooden shacks built for them after their expulsion from Thule. At the time of writing, the compensation had not been paid.

T here can be no return to the old life. The *qallunaat's* damage is done.

The Inuit cannot divorce themselves from the modern ways of the world, or from the nuclear age. Tens of thousands of Inuit, Sami and other arctic dwellers are more secure now than they have ever been. Survival is no longer a central issue. The Inuit no longer face starvation. Materially, if not spiritually, there has been a vast improvement in their lives.

Improved housing and health facilities, and lower infant mortality, have increased their numbers, but game stocks are no longer sufficient to support their hunting traditions. In truth, few indigenous northern dwellers would wish to face the rigours of the past. Softened by southern comfort and welfare, it is unlikely that the young are tough enough to live off the land and endure the hardships suffered by their ancestors. The hunting culture, and with it the old customs, will disappear.

The danger is that the peoples of the north will become human animals in a cultural zoo, mere objects of curiosity for adventurous southerners wealthy enough to enjoy the temptations of glossy travel magazines, luxury cruises through the icebergs, reindeer round-ups or photographic safaris among walrus and polar bears. For £1,000, travel agents in London sell tours of East Greenland, during which travellers are encouraged to 'experience the unique world of icebergs and glaciers, gasp at magnificent landscapes of snow-clad mountains, cross majestic frozen white lakes on skis and try the marvellous time-worn way of travel by husky dog sledge.'

American hunter. Author's photograph

Perpetuating the images of Nanook, the Midnight Sun and Europe's Last

Great Wilderness, travel promoters talk excitedly about tourism in the north, which they say is at last taking off. Flying supersonically, Concorde used to transport day trippers from Britain to Christmas lunch with the 'Lapps' in Samiland. After roaring into Rovaniemi, a medium-sized Finnish university town on the Arctic Circle, passengers who had paid £965 for the privilege were driven to a forest lodge for reindeer meat and red whortleberries, champagne and snapshots of 'Lapps' in red and blue tunics and pom-pom hats. Now that Concorde is no longer flying, other flights will surely take its place.

Reindeer round-ups and safaris are a major attraction in the Nordic countries. In winter, customers encased in thermal underwear, sweaters and down-filled anoraks don fur hats with ear muffs, are tucked snugly into individual *pulkas* and drawn across the snow-clad fells of Finland to the sound of tinkling reindeer bells. In the evenings, they relax in forest hunting lodges, luxuriate communally in saunas, and eat smoked salmon or reindeer delicacies in front of log fires of birch and pine.

Samiland's growing popularity has provided an additional source of income in an area of high unemployment. The Nordic Council, hoping to create more jobs, wants to study and breed wolves and bears, lynxes and rare arctic species at a zoo exhibiting 600 animals. The guides and ticket collectors would doubtless be Sami in traditional costume.

Herdsmen in Norway and Sweden, where tourism is more highly developed, would prefer tighter controls on visitors, who tramp over the vegetation and frighten the reindeer, often when the cows are giving birth or gaining weight for winter. A common complaint is that tourists drive too quickly. Intent on reaching the North Cape to see the midnight sun, they hurriedly photograph a passing Sami or buy a pair of reindeer boots, but show little interest in Sami culture. 'When tourists come here,' the herders say, 'they look at us like animals on a reservation.'

In the Canadian Arctic, the impact of tourism is equally disturbing. The government of the Northwest Territories, which publishes a 98-page *Official Explorers' Guide* listing available package tours, proudly observes that in ten years the number of guest lodges and outfitters has doubled. Today, the government is spending nearly a million dollars a year to promote the region in the United States and Europe.

Tourists can fish and hunt at Great Bear Lake, back-pack on Baffin Island or travel for ten days with a dog team on the sea ice ofFoxe Basin. Drum dancing, 'igloo' building and dog teams are available at a price $150 an hour at Grise Fiord on Ellesmere Island.

Sledge party, Wellington Channel
Author's photograph

For $8,500 (U.S.), tour operators offer a week-long package which includes a snowmobile trip to Beechey Island, four days' camping on Ellesmere Island, and an insufferably boring sixteen-hour return flight for the questionable bonus of a thirty-minute stopover at the North Pole for photographs and champagne. Pilots try to land within ten miles of the Pole, but weather or ice conditions may impose restrictions. As there is nothing but ice at the Pole, the photographs could just as well be taken one mile from Resolute Bay.

Throughout the Arctic, the volume of air traffic is increasing dramatically. Airlines fly polar routes to save time and fuel. Helicopters, light aircraft and Twin Otters from forty Canadian air charter companies continually ferry personnel and supplies. Pilots swoop down on animals so that tourists can photograph them, or scientists spray them with paint. Snow geese feeding in the Mackenzie Delta before migrating south may take fright at low-flying light aircraft and leave the Arctic prematurely. Unable to build up sufficient reserves of fat, they die before reaching their destinations.

Providing they are paid the going rate, Inuit on snowmobiles will tow visitors over the ice in a *U-doo*, a sledge covered with plywood and perspex, to hunt seals. (The word was first used by Bezal Jesudason in Resolute Bay, who explained: 'It is just something "U-doo" to give the passenger more protection from windchill when the sledge is towed by Ski-doos, which are much faster than dogs.') Gone are the days when an Inuk sat for 36 hours patiently waiting for his quarry to appear at a blowhole.

Now, young Inuit spy a seal basking on the ice, gun the engines of their Nordic or Yamaha snowmobiles, race at top speed towards it, and are frustrated to find that the seal has taken fright and slipped quietly into the depths. For every kill, old rifles and poor marksmanship account for a second seal which slithers wounded beneath the ice, probably to die underwater.

Without thought for the susceptibility of the game, one tourist company plans to ferry American and Japanese tourists to the icefloes off Canada's Atlantic coast. Here, they will be able to photograph the harp seal pups which, prior to animal rights campaigns, were clubbed to death for their fur by white hunters. With equal insensitivity, Canada's *Official Explorers' Guide* proclaims that 'caribou, polar bears, grizzlies, seals and whales can all be seen by lucky travellers.' Ensuring that these visitors receive value for money, Inuit snowmobiles buzz like angry wasps across the snow, round up herds of musk oxen and drive them towards the waiting bands of photographers. Knowing that polar bears can be frightened by the noise of snowmobile engines, Inuit guides illegally chase them for miles, until the exhausted bears amble placidly past the battery of tripods and long lenses.

Clearly, visitors must be primed about the possible consequences of their actions *before* they embark on journeys through the Arctic. The tide of tourism cannot be stemmed but, approached wisely, it can provide jobs and generate income without disrupting local communities or wildlife. If the sole motive for developing arctic tourism is instant profit, the result can only be an environmental disaster.

The future development of the Arctic cannot be halted. It is too late for that. Industrial man is here to stay, but the exploration and exploitation of natural resources cannot be allowed to advance unchecked. It should be subjected to stricter controls. Industry, too, needs to undergo a change of heart, and channel as much energy into the conservation of the environment, as it has, until now, into its rape.

The assessment of environmental damage from a single oil rig is meaningless when it is obvious that if oil is discovered, dozens of wells will be sunk, pipelines built, and motor and air traffic increased throughout the region. Future estimates of possible damage should be examined in the light of the harm inflicted in the past, with assessments based on completed projects, rather than on their isolated features.

Every industrial scheme in the Arctic, including the extraction of oil, should be separately mapped, with yearly additions on transparent film. At a glance, the annual rate of industrial expansion could be assessed, and where necessary curtailed. It is ludicrous to fell vast areas of forest in order to provide short-term employment.

Hydro-electric plants which have an adverse effect on reindeer pastoralism may provide cheap electricity for the cities of the South, but the resulting loss of livelihood among the Sami could incur, for the Nordic governments, infinitely greater expense in social welfare and job-creation schemes. The transportation of oil and natural gas through Baffin Bay, in the event of an accident, may result in astronomical costs for cleaning operations, legal battles and compensation. The benefits of the oil shipments would indeed be short-lived if Greenland's shrimp beds and cod fishing grounds were contaminated, and the population along the west coast had to be evacuated.

Profitability and political expediency can no longer be the only deciding factors. It is nonsensical to grant oil exploration permits on the basis of environmental assessments compiled by the industrial groups applying for them, in which government agencies may have a financial stake; it is also an insult to the public intelligence.

Applications for every development in the Arctic need reviewing by councils of independent experts drawn from industry, commerce, government and opposition parties, and ecological and conservation organisations. Their recommendations should be binding, subject to appeal through the courts. Changes can be achieved only through public awareness of the complex issues involved, and by intensifying pressure to such a degree on those in positions of authority that it becomes more expedient to heed the warnings, than to ignore them. Most of all, justice demands that the peoples whose homelands are affected should have a voice - and a decisive one - in such councils.

Government and industry can no longer pretend that wildlife preserves are none of their business. Protection of the arctic environment is everybody's business. The Canadian government ought to be publicly castigated for its dogged refusal to establish nature reserves.

T   he total acreage of the 151 sites suggested as wildlife sanctuaries by the International Biological Programme is infinitesimal in comparison with the vastness of the Arctic. Yet, in contrast to the hundreds of exploration and exploitation permits issued to oil companies, the extent of the Canadian government's concern for the environment has gone no further than to establish two national parks, which will promote tourism, and to impose a temporary moratorium on drilling in the Lancaster Sound.

This sound is an essential part of the ecological food chain in Baffin Bay and Davis Strait. For countless marine and land mammals, and millions of sea birds, lit is one of the most important breeding grounds and migration routes in the High Arctic. As the entrance to the Northwest Passage, it is equally significant for international shipping. Panarctic Oils, in which the Canadian government has a sizeable stake, proposes to ship crude oil through this channel, where other companies already have long-standing applications for permission to drill wildcat oil wells.

Hard decisions will have to be made to resolve the conflict of interests, and thought given to the advisability, rather than the feasibility, of oil shipments and of drilling in waters so unpredictable that there are years when the ice does not break up. Until all the available evidence is collated, past damage and future risks assessed, the Department of Indian Affairs and Northern Development (DIAND) in Canada should impose on all developments, for a minimum of twenty years, an immediate moratorium.

That is one solution. If it is accepted, there are many during this time who may feel that greater benefit would be achieved by establishing industrial and tourist parks, rather than wildlife reserves. This scheme is already in operation on a small scale in Finland. Here, national parkland is divided into three zones. Tourists are restricted to specific sightseeing areas, where amenities for barbecues and camping are provided, and trails clearly marked. In the 'wilderness' zones, strict regulations govern camping and hunting, and there are no organised hiking services. The 'natural' zone, by far the largest of the three, is sealed off and retained in its original state.

Industry and tourism in the Arctic could be contained in the same way within designated pockets of activity, beyond which only aboriginal hunting, research and emergency work would be permitted. Organisations such as Greenpeace and the World Wildlife Fund have an enormous contribution to make in achieving such a goal. The 'Save the Seals' campaign is destroying the livelihood of thousands of Inuit hunters. Less than ten per cent of the seals taken by Canadian Inuit are the harp seals pictured in the anti-sealing campaigns, which so effectively destroyed the European fur market.

Hoping to counter the disastrous effects for the hunters, a new international organisation, Indigenous Survival International (ISI), has been constituted. Its purpose is to defend the traditional harvesting activities of indigenous peoples, and to develop a comprehensive arctic environmental strategy which can be used as a guideline by governments and industry. Hitherto, conservationists have balked at the intricacy of the Arctic ecology and its development. A 'Save the Arctic' campaign now would be an admirable way for the animal rights groups to redeem themselves.

The need for such a campaign is urgent. Now that Nunavut is a reality, and the Inuit have greater responsibility for the management of northern resources, they must be given the capability to conduct, and profit from, research without which no amount of campaigning will save the Arctic. Science can serve the northern populations, but greater mutual advantage will stem from their full involvement in basic research, which properly funded, should be expanded to provide improved facilities for applied research.

The Arctic is of significance to every country in the northern hemisphere, and plays an indispensable role in global climatic patterns. Yet, little is known about the exchange of energy between the sea, the ice and the atmosphere. The downward movement of cold water in the arctic oceans appears to be the only truly effective mechanism for removing carbon dioxide from the atmosphere, but unless there is a more profound understanding of such processes, it will be impossible to calculate how much atmospheric pollution the oceans can safely absorb. Nor can we discover the degree of change pollutants are likely to cause to the climate of Europe and North America, or whether the icecaps will melt. Who better to study such mysteries than the Inuit?

I   nvestigation into the microscopic organisms which adapt so success-fully to the arctic cold, the long winter darkness and the continual summer daylight may produce information which will directly benefit human health. Understanding the natural biorhythms of animals in the polar regions may assist us in judging human reactions to arctic conditions, and help to create working routines to improve productivity. Extensive programmes need to be undertaken to find ways to minimise noise in offshore developments, and to reduce the impact of pipelines, causeways and roads.

The most pressing task for researchers is to find new ways of reducing to zero the industrial emissions of sulphur dioxide and air pollutants, to investigate the long-range transportation of soot and chemicals, and evaluate the dangers of climatic changes as a result of burning fossil fuels. Man needs to know what are the prevailing physical and chemical conditions in the North Atlantic and Arctic Oceans, into which falls the bulk of the industrial pollution of Europe and North America. The causes and potential effects of unexpectedly high levels of heavy metals in marine mammals off the coast of Greenland require urgent attention.

Industrial emissions must be reduced at a quickening pace, in view of the industrial expansion in Siberia. The British government will have to join the rest of Europe and sign the Helsinki Protocol on sulphur dioxide emissions, or take rapid action against those industries which produce the contaminants.

International cooperation is solving the problems of the Arctic, and the mutual exchange of information, will provide excellent opportunities for dispelling some of the mistrust between east and west. American and Canadian expertise in business and management techniques could be pooled with Soviet advances in metal welding, building processes, and plant and vegetable breeding. Each nation with territory north of the 66th parallel, assisted by the indigenous populations, should formulate an arctic policy in which protection of the land and its peoples is paramount.

The makers of arctic policy ought to give greater responsibility to northern peoples, who have no wish to live in the past, and no desire to be mere objects of southern curiosity. Now is the time to help to restore their confidence and pride. The Inuit and the Sami harbour no secret longings to threaten the sovereignty of the Canadian or Nordic governments. Their goal is to control the new developments, and to guarantee the future growth of their cultures. The Canadian government is to be commended for beginning the process of negotiating native claims, and for lending millions of dollars to the Inuit to fight their cause. What is required now is to nurture the Inuit's self-respect.

Inuit organisations have already shown themselves to be responsible, politically astute bodies. Decisions on resource development, tourism, housing, employment and social policies should be taken with their participation. Involvement in these issues will provide local people with the necessary training before they shoulder their full responsibilities.

Inuit kayaker, Illulisaat Glacier, Greenland.

Author's photograph

The Inuit communities should be given their fair share of the royalties from oil, gas and minerals. They could be channelled into health and education, social and economic projects and small-scale industries for the arctic market. Local ventures will motivate the Inuit, and provide work in each community for those who cannot hunt. Initially, government subsidies may be required, but hand-outs tend to promote discontent and a sense of hopelessness. Far better that Inuit projects are funded with income from generous royalties and land-claim settlements, while government finance is used to support research into improving arctic productivity. .

Soviet scientists have shown that the potential for agriculture and horticulture in the north is greater than is generally supposed. One day, millions *of* acres *of* arable land in the Mackenzie Valley and the Yukon will be ploughed to grow grain and root crops. In time, each community in the north will be self-sufficient in fruit and vegetables, eggs, milk and a variety *of* nutritious foods. Shrimp, arctic char and seafood products can be harvested and exported to the south, earning millions *of* dollars a year. Commercial fisheries and vegetable farms will cut the crippling costs of transportation, and help to improve diet.

If tomatoes and cabbages which are resistant to the cold can be grown larger in Siberia than on the banks of the Volga, the Inuit of Grise Fiord, Resolute Bay and Pond Inlet should not have to pay for fresh supplies to be flown in from Edmonton.

The opportunities are limitless. Musk oxen can be bred and farmed for their lightweight wool, which is in great demand in the south. In Asia, where powdered elephant and rhinoceros tusks are sold as aphrodisiacs, there are ready markets for caribou and reindeer antlers, which are renewed annually.

The oil industry could make a valuable contribution by providing, in part payment of royalties and development taxes, transport for raw materials, and surplus heat for technical schools and workshops - an insurance for the Inuit. They could then harness their adaptive and inventive abilities, sell their arts and crafts, manufacture clothing, footwear, furniture and pre-moulded goods, and each community would specialise in its own product or products.

The requirement for achieving these dreams is political will. Conservation of the north, and the helping hand which has to be extended to its peoples, will prove to be expensive. The Arctic- is too important to be ignored. It is our heritage, and should be preserved for future generations. From now on, the Inuit and the *qallunaat* must work together, as partners.

EPILOGUE

Climate change is melting polar ice to such a rapid extent that polar bears are being separated from their principal source of food, the seal.   *Author's photograph*

Without question, the greatest current threat to the arctic regions is the increasingly rapid melting of the polar ice, probably caused by global warming. Scientists now believe that the ice that covers the Arctic Ocean is shrinking so swiftly that the entire ocean could someday be ice-free during the summer months -- a transformation that could alter everything from world shipping routes to the fate of winter wheat crops in Kansas. Although the Arctic ice pack varies rapidly with the seasons, climate researchers say that the area covered by perennial ice -- that which remains from year to year -- reached a record low level in 2003, a phenomenon that is likely to be repeated. Frighteningly, NASA satellite images show that Arctic ice has been shrinking at the rate of nearly 10 percent a decade. During the past 35 years, it also has thinned by more than 40 percent -- from 9 feet thick to about 5 feet. This will almost certainly jeopardise the ecology of the entire Arctic and the feeding grounds of many large whales. The bowhead, narwhal, and beluga, which live in Arctic waters year-round, are in particular danger.

Climate change may also impact the areas of the oceans in which whales live, including migration patterns. Climate change, depletion in the ozone layer and the related rise in UV radiation may also lead to a fall in the population of krill, a primary food source for many marine species.

Polar bears similarly are reportedly finding it difficult to reach their prime source of food, the seal, because there is now much less ice, which in turn restrains their migration habits.

Two eminent British scientists from the Scott Polar Research Institute in Cambridge, Dr Peter Wadhams and Dr. Norman Davis, have calculated that the ice in the Fram Strait, between Svalbard and Greenland, thinned by *forty three per cent* in the past two decades. This is frightening because of the potentially serious implications for climates at high latitudes.

Moreover, this rapid and extensive thinning agrees with results published last year by Drew Rothrock, of the University of Washington, for thinning from the North Pole to the Bering Strait. This was measured by US submarines at approximately the same time and thus confirms that the thinning of sea ice is indeed Arctic-wide.

Michael Steele, senior oceanographer at the University of Washington, Seattle, says that warming trends like those found in these studies could greatly affect ocean processes, which, in turn, impact Arctic and global climate. Liquid water absorbs the Sun's energy rather than reflecting it into the atmosphere the way ice does. As the oceans warm and ice thins, more solar energy is absorbed by the water, creating positive feedbacks that lead to further melting.

Such dynamics can change the temperature of ocean layers, impact ocean circulation and salinity, change marine habitats, and widen shipping lanes, Steele says.

In related NASA-funded research that observes perennial sea-ice trends, Mark C. Serreze, a scientist at the University of Colorado, Boulder, found that in 2002 the extent of Arctic summer sea ice reached the lowest level in the satellite record, suggesting this is part of a trend. "In the summer if 2003, we have not seen a recovery. In fact, we are reinforcing the general downward trend." Indeed, another study shows that the rate of warming in the Arctic over the last 20 years is eight times the rate of warming over the last 100 years.

I n 2003, the largest ice shelf in the Arctic, the Ward Hunt Shelf which has been in place for 3,000 years, broke into two pieces, each one riddled with fissures. As it did so, an entire freshwater lake drained into the ocean.

This follows hard on the heels of the breakup of the 3,250 square kilometre Larsen B ice shelf. In Antarctica. In one month, it shattered into thousands of icebergs.

One result of all this is that as the high latitudes warm, and the extent of the sea ice declines,   thawing Arctic soils are releasing significant amounts of carbon dioxide and methane now trapped in the permafrost, the soil that used to stay frozen all year round. The permafrost has acted as a carbon sink, locking away carbon and other greenhouse gases like methane, for thousands of years. Now, in some areas, it is beginning to give back its carbon.

About 14% of the carbon stored in the world's soils is estimated to be in the Arctic. This probably amounts to several hundred Gigatonnes, and the release of the entire Arctic carbon store, if it happened, would add prodigiously to climate change (emissions of all greenhouse gases produced by human activities are about six Gt annually).

The permafrost is normally ideal for construction, because of its solidity, but studies at the University of Alaska at Fairbanks suggest that a warming of the permafrost from minus four to minus one degree Celsius decreases its load-bearing capacity by up to 70%.

Damage to buildings, roads, pipelines and other structures caused by thawing of the permafrost is already occurring in Alaska and Siberia. The Intergovernmental Panel on Climate Change is now also suggesting that global average temperatures might increase by 2100 by up to 5.8 degrees Celsius. In high latitudes, the worst case could be almost twice that.

This is because as the temperature increases, the snow cover will move northwards, and the soil that is then exposed will be very slow to revegetate. As a result, it will absorb more solar energy. Consequently, anybody planning to invest in a ski resort in, say, Norway will need to put their money higher up the mountain: the Norwegian skiing season is already getting shorter.

Similarly, climate change together with other negative influences constitutes a serious threat to an estimated 200,000 indigenous people, from 30 ethnic groups, in the Russian Arctic, and for similar groups elsewhere in the permafrost zone, whose very existence is endangered.

In the last four decades, the Arctic ice has lost 40% of its volume. Clearly, we must to learn to adapt, but having spent years studying the arctic regions, I cannot help but wonder – would our efforts not be better directed at trying to force indolent and self-serving politicians and bureaucrats to *act* rather than talk?

For none of us should ever forget that the Arctic is *our* heritage.

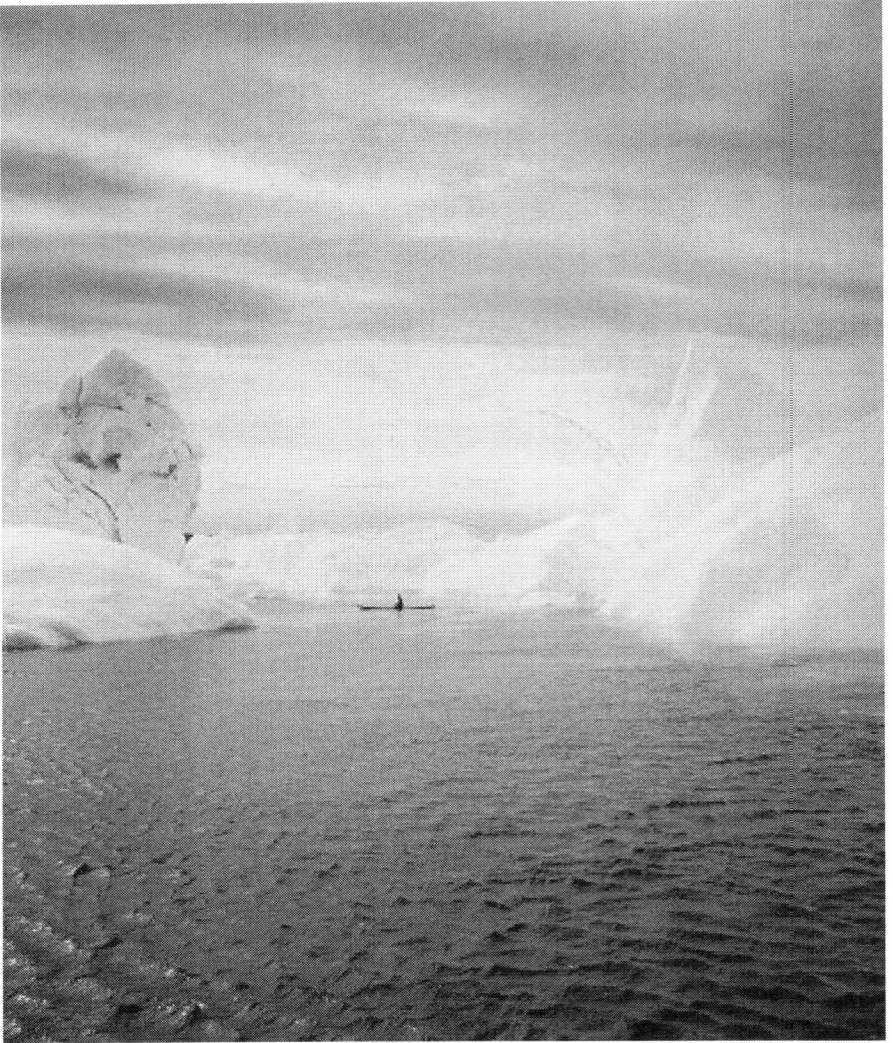

Our Heritage   *Author's photograph*

ACKNOWLEDGMENTS

This book would not have been written had it not been for Vernon Mann, a reporter for Independent Television News (I TN) Ltd., in London, who, as duty Foreign Editor in May, 1983, assigned me to cover the voyage of a replica Viking ship across the North Sea. Before the passage was successfully completed, we twice lost a steering oar, and were towed a hundred miles back to shore in a Force Eight wind, in constant danger of capsizing owing to an insecure mast.

I was in expert hands, however. The skipper of *Saga Siglar*, Ragnar Thorseth, had previously crossed the North Sea in a canoe, sailed through the Northwest Passage in a cabin cruiser, and with my cameraman, Trygve Berge, in 1982 had become the first Norwegian to reach the North Pole. With Max Vinner of the Vikingeskibsmuseet in Vanloese, Denmark, who extended unlimited moral support during the voyage, they stirred a latent interest in the Vikings, and introduced me to Eiriksfjord and the Viking settlements in Greenland.

In Nuuk, I was fortunate to meet and befriend Philip Lauritzen, then the Head of Information for Greenland's Home Rule government. More than anyone, he opened up for me an arctic world, of which I knew nothing. My thanks are also due to Jan Drent and Ole Heinrich at Tusarliivik, Fleming Christenssen and his colleagues at the Ice Patrol headquarters at Narssarssuaq, and Peter Lind, for his gargantuan efforts in re-arranging my travel plans at 24 hours' notice.

Moses Olsen, Greenland's Deputy Prime Minister, and Dr Robert Petersen, the renowned eskimologist, deserve special thanks for their time and help, and for the valuable insights they gave me into the psychological and political background of the Greenlanders. The same applies to Joseph Motzfeldt, who shared with me his remaining food and offered me lodging during the process of leaving his home in Uummaannaq, prior to taking up his new position as Greenland's Minister of Education in Nuuk. I am equally grateful to the management of Greenex *MS*, who helicoptered me hundreds of miles across Greenland, and welcomed me to stay at the Black Angel Mine at

Marmoriliik, which they have since closed down.

The hospitality of Bezal, now deceased, and Terry Jesudason in Resolute Bay is well known among arctic travellers, and during the writing of this book my thoughts have frequently returned to them. I am also grateful to Dennis Hillman of the Baffin Cooperative Society, Jamie MacKendrick, Senior Development Officer of the NWT government in Yellowknife, Rev. Jim Bell of Baffin Island, and to the staff of The Inuit Circumpolar Conference, DIAND, the Canadian Wildlife Service, the Resolute Weather Bureau and the RCMP. Although far too numerous to mention individually, hundreds of officials, oil workers and Inuit throughout the Arctic gave me their time and hospitality during nearly three years' research. Special mention must be made of Tony Manik and Larry Audlaluk at Resolute, who taught me so much, and Paul Kasudluak and Elijah Nutarra (E.9912) of Grise Fiord, whose soapstone carvings are a constant reminder of our times together on the ice.

I would like to acknowledge my debt to my good friend of more than twenty years' standing in Scandinavia, Mr Tom Soederman of the Finnish Foreign Ministry and Mr Lasse Lehtinen at the London Embassy. Another great 'Finnfriend', is Mr Matti Kohva, of Finnfacts in Helsinki, with whom I shared many happy saunas and struggled through the snows of Samiland in search of reindeer and Finnish soldiers. Mr Teuvo Tikkanen, also of Finnfacts, and Captain Tom Artela offered unlimited assistance during our sub-zero voyage on board the icebreaker, *Urho*. I am indebted to Mr Tankmar Horn, the Chairman of Wartsila Shipyard in Helsinki, Mr Harri Soininen, the manager for Wartsila Consulting Engineering and Mr Goran Wilkman, the Head of Wartsila's Arctic Research Centre. Their expertise and patience with my naive questions was invaluable. Thanks are also due to Oystein Dalland and Philip Hayes, in Norway, for their assistance on the Alta affair. Among the Sami, Aslak Magga, Maaret-Anne and Inga Magga deserve special mention.

In Britain, Sir David Nicholas, the former Editor of ITN, was generous in allowing me several weeks off work to travel to the High Arctic. I should also like to express my warmest thanks to Jim Green, Ian Lomas, Mike Chandler, John Davies, and Ian Aldridge, Bob Learmonth, Doug Fenner, John Wroe and Stuart Maskell, of ITN's News Information Library, who helped me to find elusive details on a variety of subjects. Mrs. Pam Barlow at The Society for Cultural Relations with the USSR, was equally tireless in her efforts to assist. Additionally, my knowledge of birdlife improved greatly with the assistance of the late ornithologist, Mr Roger Durman, who took such an interest in my project and checked the manuscript for factual errors.

To my dear wife, my love and thanks for living with my obsession, for enduring my depressive moods when words would not come or my word processor failed, for helping to acquire books long out of print, and for understanding my need to travel in such inhospitable regions.

My warmest thanks go also to her mother, Mrs Marion Higgins, who not only corrected the manuscript, but with infinite patience, kindness and wisdom taught me discipline in language, and showed me the difference between writing for television news and for a publisher. Without her invaluable help and encouragement, this first book might never have been completed.

Above all others, my thanks go to the Inuit, the Sami and the peoples of the North.

S.H.

Permissions

P ermission to quote from the Hudson's Bay Record Society volumes has been received from the Keeper, Hudson's Bay Company Archives, provincial Archives of Manitoba. Permission to quote from Jean Malaurie, *The Last Kings of Thule*, has come from Messrs Jonathan Cape and E. P. Dutton (English translation @ 1982 by Jonathan Cape and E. P. Dutton). Permission to quote from Robert E. Peary, *The Discovery of the North Pole*, has come from Messrs Hodder & Stoughton. To all of these grateful thanks.

GLOSSARY

Angakok - Wise man of a settlement, a spiritual leader. Plural: **Angakut. Arnarkuagssoq** - Goddess of the Sea, another name for **Sedna.**

Iglu - Stone and turf house.
Ilisiitok - Evil old man or woman. Plural: **Ilisiituk.**
Illuliaq - Traditional 'igloo'.

Inua - A soul, which the Inuit believed possessed all animate beings and inanimate objects.

Inuk - An 'eskimo'. The work means 'human being', a 'real man'. Plural: **Inuit.**
Inuit - Plural form of Inuk.
Inuktitut - Language spoken by Inuit.
Inuvialuit - Inuit living in the Mackenzie Delta region.
Joiking - Sami style of singing, very similar to that of the Inuit.

Kamiks - Boots of skin, often thigh length.

Kayak - Slender boat used for hunting at sea, made of seal skin stretched over
   bone or wooden framework. In Eurasia, known as **baidar.**
Knarr - Viking merchant ship.

Mattak, Muktut - The skin of walrus, whale or narwhal. A delicacy rich in protein and

vitamins.
Nanuuk - A polar bear.
Nerrivik - Another name for **Sedna**. Also **Neqiviq.**
Nunavut - The territory containing all land and sea north of the tree line, east of the Mackenzie River, claimed by the Inuit as their homeland, governed by themselves within the Canadian Confederation under the super vision of Ottawa.
Polynya - An open channel of water.

Pulka - A small, boat-like sledge used by the **Sami**. Also known as an **akya** or **keris.**

Qallunaat - Inuit term for 'white man'. Also known as **Kabloonah.**
Qivitok - Half-savage victims of **Ilisiituk**, living wild in the mountains.

Sami , Samer, Sameh - The people of Samiland, formerly called 'Lapps'.

Sedna - Goddess of the Sea and marine life. The most powerful of all the influences on the Inuit, with the exception of **Sila.**

Shaman - Spiritual leader, wise man of a settlement, also known as an   **angakok.**

Sila - A spiritual presence, similar to the Chinese Tao. The most influential God in the Inuit world.
Skraelingar - Derogatory Viking word for the Inuit.
Tomat - Ministering spirits used by **angakut.**

Tupilak - Spirit, ghost. Plural: **Tupilek.**

Ulu - Woman's 'u'-shaped knife, used for flensing seal.

Umiak - Communal boat of skin, capable of carrying 10-12 people.

BIBLIOGRAPHY

During the past thirty years, hundreds of books have been written about the Arctic. The following is a selective bibliography of the most important titles. Each one will assist the reader to delve more deeply into specific aspects of the North.

Almgren, Bertil, and others. *The Viking*. AB Nordbok, Sweden, 1975.

Armstrong, Terence (with Brian Roberts, Charles Swithinbank). *Illustrated Glossary of Snow and /ce*. Scott Polar Research Institute, Cambridge, 1973.

Asp, Erkki. *The Lapps and the Lappish Culture*. University of Turku, Finland,1980.

   The Social Consequences of Regulating the Watercourses in Lapland. University of Turku, Finland, 1981.

   The Skolt Lapps. University ofTurku, Finland, 1982.

Baker, Dr Robin. *The Mystery of Migration*. Macdonald Futura Books, London,1980.

Bhardarson, Ivar. *Det gamle Groenlands beskrivelse*. Ed. Finnur Jonsson, Copenhagen, 1930.

Berger, Thomas R. *Northern Frontier, Northern Homeland*. The Report of the Mackenzie Valley Pipeline Inquiry. Supply & Services Canada, Ottawa, 1977.

Birket-Smith, Kaj. *The Caribou Eskimos*. Nordisk Forlag, Copenhagen, 1940.

   Anthropological Observations on the Central Eskimos. Nordisk Forlag, Copenhagen, 1940.

Brower, Mayor Eugene. Address to Alaska Science Conference, Whitehorse, NWT. Sept., 1983.

Canadian Arctic Resources Committee (CARC). *Northern Perspectives*. Ottawa, no date.

Chantraine, Pol. *The Living /ce*. McClelland & Stewart, Toronto, 1980.

Creery, Ian. *The Inuit of Canada*. The Minority Rights Group, London, 1983.

Crisler, Lois. *Arctic Wild*. Secker & Warburg, London, 1959.

Cummings, Peter. *Canada: Native Land Rights and Northern Development*. IWGIA Document 26. Copenhagen, 1977.

Dalland, Oystein. *The Alta Case - Learning from the Errors Made in a Human Ecological Conflict in Norway*. Pergamon Press Ltd, London, 1983.

Danish Ministry for Greenland. *Groenland, 1982*. Arsberetning, Copenhagen, 1983.

Degerbol, Magnus. 'Animal Bones from the Norse Ruins at Gardar'. *Meddelser om Groenland* 76,3, p. 183 44. Copenhagen, 1929.

Dene Nation, The. *Denendeh*. The Dene Nation, Yellowknife, 1984.

DIAND. *Government Activities in the North*, 1982-83.

Lancaster Sound Region,1980-2000, The. Government Green Paper, Ottawa, 1982.

Dyson,John. *The Hot Arctic*. Heinemann, London, 1979.

Egede, Hans. *Det gamle Groenlands nye Perlustration eller Naturel-Historie etc.*1741. ed. Louis Bob. *Meddelser om Groenland*, 54, Copenhagen, 1925. *Relationer fra Groenland* 1721-1736, ed. Louis Bob, *Meddelserom Groenland*,54, Copenhagen, 1925. *Efterretninger om Groenland*, Copenhagen, ca. 1725.

Egede, Poul. *Relationer fra Groenland*, 1741. *Meddelser om Groenland*, 54, Copenhagen, 1925. *Efterretninger om Groenland*, Copenhagen, ca. 1725.

Emmelin, Lars. Address, Nordic Scientific Conference, Ny Alesund, Svalbard, August, 1984.

Freuchen, Peter. *Arctic Adventure: My Life in the Frozen North*. Wm. Heinemann Ltd, London, 1936. *Book of the Eskimos*. The World Publishing Co, Cleveland, 1951.

Gad, Finn. *The History of Greenland*. Vol. I, II: C. Hurst & Co, London, 1970, 1973. Vol III: Nytt Nordisk Forlag, Copenhagen, 1975.

Gallagher, H. G. *Etok: A Story of Eskimo Power*. Putnam, New York, 1974.

Herbert, Wally. *Eskimos.* Collins, London, 1976. *Across the Top of the World: The British Trans-Araic Expedition.* Longmans, London, 1969.

Herding, Knud (with Erik Hesselbjerg, Svend Klitgaard, Ebbe Munck, Olaf Petersen). *Greenland Past and Present.* Edvard Henriksen, Copenhagen, no date.

Hudson's Bay Record Society. *Andrew Graham's Observations on Hudson's Bay, 1767-1791,* Vol XXVII, Hudson's Bay Record Society, London, no date. *Northern Qutebec and Labrador Journals and Correspondence, 1819-1835,* Vol XXIV. No date.

Illingworth, Frank. *Wild Lift Beyond the North.* Country Life Ltd, London, 1951.

Inuit Circumpolar Conference. *The President's Report 1980-1983.* Nuuk, no date.

Inuit Tapirisat of Canada. *Inuit Nunagat - The Peoples' Land.* The Inuit Land Claims Commission,

Ottawa, 1978. *Nunavut, Agreement in Principle Between the Guvernment and the Inuit Tapirisat of Canada.* Ottawa, 1976. *Inuit Today,* and *ITC News.*

Irwin, Colin. 'Inuit Navigation, Empirical Reasoning and Survival'. *Journal of Navigation,* May, 1985.

Jacobi, Hans. *Usukutaq.* Jakobshavn Turistforening, Greenland, no date.

Jones, Mervyn. *The Sami of Lapland.* The Minority Rights Group, London, 1982.

Kaalund, Bodil. *The Art of Greenland.* University of California Press, Berkeley, 1983.

Keating, Bern. *The Northwest Passage.* Rand McNally & Co, Chicago, 1970.

Lauritzen, Philip. *Oil and Amulets.* Breakwater Books, Stjohn's, 1983.

Lipton, Barbara. *Survival: Life and Art of the Alaskan Eskimo.* Newark Museum and Morgan and Morgan, New York, 1977.

Livingston, John. *Arctic Oil.* Canadian Broadcasting Corporation, Toronto, 1981.

Magnusson, Magnus. *Viking Expansion Westwards.* The Bodley Head, London, 1973.

Malaurie, Jean. *The Last Kings of Thule.* Jonathan Cape, London, 1982. E. P. Dutton, New York, 1982.

Manker, Ernst. *People of Eight Seasons.* AB Nordbok, Sweden, 1975.

Markham, Albert Hastings. *A Whaling Cruise to Baffin's Bay.* Sampson Low, Marston, Low & Searle, London, 1875.

Marsden, Walter. *Lapland.* Time-Life International, Amsterdam, 1976.

Mauss, Marcel. *Seasonal Variations of the Eskimo.* Routledge & Kegan Paul, London, 1979.

Marchuk, Guri. *Science and Siberia.* Novosti Press Agency, Moscow, 1983.

Mead, W. R. (with Helmer Smeds). *Winter in Finland.* Hugh Evelyn Ltd, London, 1967.

Milne, Allen R. (with Brian D. Smiley). *Offshore Drilling in Lancaster Sound: Possible Environmental Hazards.* Canadian Dept. of Fisheries and Environment, Sidney, B.c., 1978.

Mowat, Farley. *Sea of Slaughter.* McClelland & Stewart, Toronto, 1984.

Nansen, Fritjiof. *Eskimo Life.* Longmans, Green & Co, London, 1894.

National Geographic Society. *Alaska: High Roads to Adventure.* Washington, D.C., 1976. *Alaska's Magnificent Parklands.* Washington, D.C., 1984.

Olivant, Simon. *Arctic Challenge to NATO.* The Institute for the Study of Conflict, London, 1985.

Paine, Robert. *Dam a River, Damn a People?* International Work Group for Indigenous Affairs (IWGIA), Copenhagen, 1982.

Peary, Robert E. *Nearest the Pole.* Hutchinson & Co, London, 1907. *The Discovery of the North Pole.* Hodder & Stoughton, London, 1910.

Petersen, H. C. *Instruction in Kayak Building.* Vikingeskibshallen, Roskilde, Copenhagen Groenlands

Landsmuseum, no date.

Pimlott, Douglas. *Oil under the ice - Offshore Drilling in the Canadian Arctic.* Canadian Arctic Resources Committee (CARC), Ottawa, 1976.

Rasmussen, Knud. *Across Arctic America: Narrative of the Fifth Thule Expedition.*Greenwood Press, New York, no date.

Rawlins, Dennis. *Peary at the Pole: Fact or Fiction?* R. B. Luce, Washington, 1973.

Ray, Dorothy Jean. *Artists of the Tundra and the Sea.* University of Washington Press, Seattle, 1961.

Resnick, Abraham. *Siberia and the Soviet Far East: Endless Frontiers.* Novosti Press Agency, Moscow, 1983.

Rich, E. E. *Hudson's Bay Company, 1670-1763,* Vol 1. Hudson's Bay Record Society, London, no date.

Ries, Tomas. 'Defending the Far North', *International Defense Review* 7 (1984).

Ritchie, Carson. *Art of the Eskimo.* A. S. Barnes & Co, South Brunswick / New York 1979. Yoseloff Ltd, London, 1979.

Scott,]. M. *Icebound.* Gordon & Cremonesi, London, 1977.

Salomonsen, Finn. *The Arctic Year.* Jonathan Cape, London, 1960.

Smith, D. Murray. *Arctic Expeditions from British and Foreign Shores.* London, ca.1877. *Early Arctic Expeditions.* London, 1877.

Smith, Frances C. *The World of the Arctic.* Lutterworth Press, London, 1960.

Smith, Norman. *The Unbelievable Land* Canadian Broadcasting Corporation. Queen's Printer, Ottawa, 1971.

Smucker, Samuel M. *Arctic Explorations and Discoveries during the Nineteenth Century.* Miller, Orton & Co, New York, 1857.

Spence, Bill. *Harpooned: The Story of Whaling.* Conway Maritime Press Ltd, Greenwich, 1980.

Steltzer, Ulli. *Inuit: The North in Transition.* Douglas & McIntyre Ltd, Vancouver/Toronto, 1982.

Taylor, Col. Wm. J., Jr. *The Challenge to Nato's Northern Flank.* USICA,Washington, no date.

Valkeapaa, Nils-Aslak. *Greetings from Lappland.* Zed Press, London, 1983.

Whymper, Frederick. *Heroes of the Arctic.* Society for Promoting Christian Knowledge, London, 1875.

Williamson, Kenneth. *Bird Study,* Vol. 22. No.2. Sept, 1975.

Printed in Great Britain
by Amazon

16100097R00059